Finding the Bull

Inside the Bear

Active Management Strategies
for *Expansions*, *Contractions*,
and *Everything* in Between

Robert N. Stein

Senior Portfolio Manager and Economist, *Astor Asset Management*

Marketplace Books
Columbia, Maryland

Publisher: Chris Myers

VP/General Manager: John Boyer

Marketing Manager: Danielle Hainsey

Senior Graphic Designer: Jennifer Marin

Graphic Designer: Beth Hall

Copyright © 2013 by Robert N. Stein

Published by Marketplace Books Inc.

All rights reserved.

ISBN: 1-59280-579-5
ISBN 13: 978-1-59280-579-2

DEDICATION

In Memory of My Father, Jerry Stein
April 5, 1929—December 5, 2011

———— ◆ ◆ ————

ACKNOWLEDGEMENTS

A simple thank you is never enough, but hopefully my heartfelt words of gratitude mentioned here will somehow express my appreciation for the support I have received from so many sources, expected and unexpected. Enough cannot be said about my good friend of 20 plus years, colleague and partner, the vice chairman of our investment committee, whose fingerprints are all over this book, our models, and our philosophy, John Eckstein.

My colleagues at Astor who work above and beyond the call of duty to give our clients the best service and products, and are truly dedicated to our cause. On the Astor Team, I wish to thank Bryan Novak, Scott Thomas, Brian Durbin, and Jaclyn Polancic. Special thanks go out to Stephanie Yuskis who is my personal GPS.

Of course, support outside of business is also very important in completing this project. My family has always been supportive of me in almost all of my endeavors; my wife, Eileen, and my son Spencer are my biggest fans.

I hope all will enjoy this book and take away from it a new understanding of the importance of active management and investment, to "find the bull inside the bear."

Thank you,
Rob Stein

TABLE OF CONTENTS

INTRODUCTION: An Investment Paradigm for Today's Economic Climate — **vii**

Reacting to the Market by Applying Active Management — ix

CHAPTER 1: Understanding the Basics of Macroeconomics-Based Investing — **1**

Defining the Business Cycle in Real Time — 2

Participating in the Broad Market — 8

Pursuing Benefits in Any Cycle — 11

CHAPTER 2: Outlook 2013—It's All About Demand — **13**

2012 Recap — 14

2013—Modest Growth with a Chance of Acceleration — 15

Deflation and Inflation—No Big Worries for 2013 — 18

Eye on the Fed — 19

Gold, Currencies, and Energy — 21

Real Estate and Housing — 24

Domestic Economic Sectors — 24

Stock and Bond Correlations — 26

International Outlook — 26

Conclusion: Slow and Steady — 27

CHAPTER 3: The Case for Tactical Asset Management — **29**

What Does Tactical Mean? — 31

A Tale of Two Tapes — 32

The Impact of Tactical Strategies — 34

The Next Cycle — 37

CHAPTER 4: ETFs and Active Management in Action   **39**

Avoiding Catastrophe   39

Praise for the ETF   41

Active Management: A Value Proposition   42

Risk and Reward   46

Why You Should Worry About Drawdowns   46

The Case Study   48

Fundamentally Weighted ETFs   50

Summary: Strategies for Tomorrow's Markets   50

ABOUT THE AUTHOR   **55**

GLOSSARY OF ECONOMIC TERMS   **59**

ECONOMIC CALENDAR   **79**

Introduction

AN INVESTMENT PARADIGM FOR TODAY'S ECONOMIC CLIMATE

We are in a new investment paradigm today. No, it is not the new normal; perhaps more like the old normal with a piano on its back. The good news—and, yes, this is good news—is "visible risk" has re-entered the market. While the notion of risk might be scary for some investors, the alternative is "complete uncertainty," and that's *really* scary. The period of uncertainty and the attempts to manage things through extensive central bank intervention, government regulation, and international drama made the market particularly challenging for fundamental tactical managers. I would rather know, or at least be able to evaluate, reduce, hedge, or accept risk, rather than fly blind with uncertainty—even if the government says it is here to help (which, according to late President Ronald Reagan, are the scariest words in the English language).

Risk, when evaluated and allocated properly, provides investors with the potential for reaping rewards for taking an appropriate amount of risk. We may not like some of the outcomes which now fall under the category of "visible risk," but knowledge of these outcomes will make us better investors.

Additionally, the risk-on, risk-off environment that can, and over the past few years has, driven equity prices up and down by double digit percentages in a short time span is fading. We see this in the correlation between stocks and bonds. Traditionally, stocks and bonds experience periods of high correlations and low correlations (meaning they move together or opposite of each other), as we have seen over time. During economic stress and uncertainty, however, they tend to be negatively correlated, which makes it very difficult to mitigate risk. Now, stocks and bonds—which both traded up in 2012—are trending back the other way with positive correlation, as the chart below illustrates.

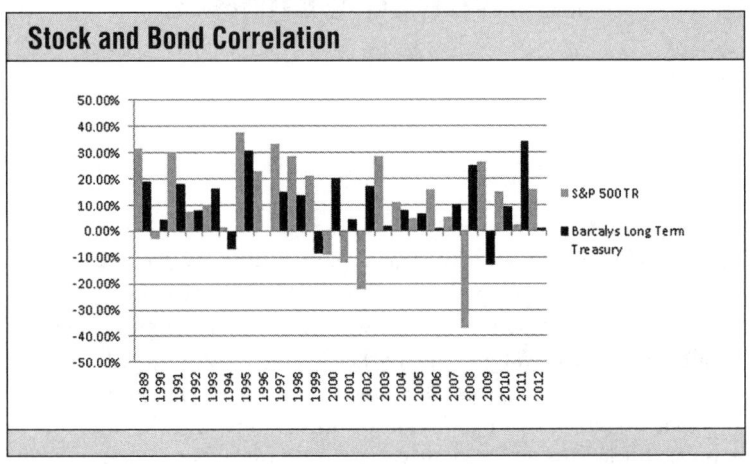

In this new investment climate, active asset management will once again play an important role. Active management means taking a pro-active approach to investing by utilizing fundamental and/or technical analysis to create value in a portfolio. This approach allows financial professionals and their clients to make profit—or at least limit losses—in any type of market climate, regardless of market direction, volatility, or bull or bear conditions.

More than ever, active management is a necessary strategy to pursue an independent and empowered financial future. For many investors, there is a tactical advantage to be gained from dedicating a portion of their assets to active management. Through active management, investors and their advisors are no longer held captive by traditional buy-

and-hold strategies, and have an important defense against the vagaries of the stock market.

At Astor Asset Management, our macroeconomics-based approach to active management means, in simplest terms, that we buy equities when the economic conditions are most favorable (economic expansion) and sell equities or even take a short position in the market when the economic conditions dictate (economic contraction). We invest based on the current economic conditions—not what we believe the economy will likely do a few months from now. Economic reality is far more powerful than a hypothetical forecast. Thus, we strive to put the power of "the big picture" behind each investment decision.

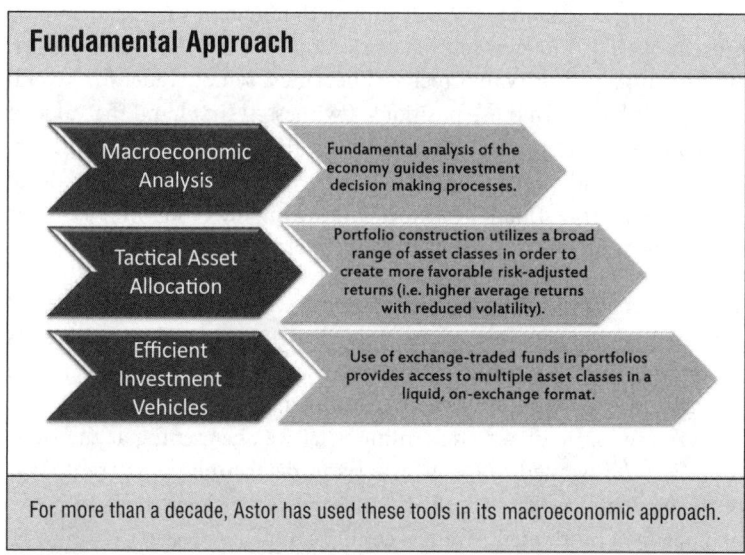

Fundamental Approach

Macroeconomic Analysis — Fundamental analysis of the economy guides investment decision making processes.

Tactical Asset Allocation — Portfolio construction utilizes a broad range of asset classes in order to create more favorable risk-adjusted returns (i.e. higher average returns with reduced volatility).

Efficient Investment Vehicles — Use of exchange-traded funds in portfolios provides access to multiple asset classes in a liquid, on-exchange format.

For more than a decade, Astor has used these tools in its macroeconomic approach.

Reacting to the Market by Applying Active Management

At Astor, we use broad fundamental indicators, such as output trends and employment trends, as tools to gauge the state of the economy. In addition to identifying and interpreting the current stage of the economic cycle—expansion, peak, contraction, and trough—we also use the proprietary Astor Economic Index to determine the state of the economy, and thus position our portfolio, as you will read further in Chapter 1.

Our research has proven that the Astor Economic Index has a high correlation to the strength and weakness of the overall economy. As we will mention numerous times throughout this book, increasing exposure to equities during positive economic environments and decreasing exposure during contracting economic fundamentals is extremely productive for portfolio construction. Through our economically driven approach, Astor has amassed a successful track record.

Over my years as an economist, I have combined an in-depth study of the economy and a passion for the markets into a single discipline: investing based on the economic cycle. I started my career as an intern at the Federal Reserve, when Paul Volcker was chairman. Part of my job was to compile economic data, dealing with tangibles such as the rate of growth of GDP, money supply statistics, the size of the U.S. workforce, etc. I then moved to Wall Street and became a senior trader for several prestigious banks. In these positions, I witnessed first hand the value of economic data. Data not only influenced the markets, but also determined the overall tone and direction of the economy. I quickly realized when making investment decisions, forecasting the economy was not as important as identifying the current stage of the economic cycle.

The problem with forecasting is that I was wrong a lot. It's like the old joke that says economists were created to make weather forecasters look good. Very quickly I returned to my analytical roots. Rather than trying to predict what was going to happen, I preferred to review and analyze economic data to determine what was happening at the time. Specifically, I wanted to create criteria to determine the current stage of the business cycle. Once the business cycle was identified, an active management investment strategy could be implemented to capitalize on a particular stage.

At Astor today, rather than making investment decisions based on market timing or predictions that typically have a low percentage of accuracy, we focus on identifying the current stage of the economic cycle—a cornerstone of our investment philosophy. There are also gradations to our long and short positions. Thus, we must be prepared, depending upon our analysis of the economy and the readings of the Astor Economic Index, for example, to be 75 to 100 percent long equities at times, and only 25 to 50 percent long at others. Or, we may take a 25 percent short position in one market, such as the Nasdaq, while retaining a long position in another, such as the S&P 500. It's all determined by vigilantly analyzing economic indicators that signal the current stage of the economy.

One finger must be kept on the pulse of the economy and another on the trigger of investment decisions. Make no mistake: I am not talking about capturing short-term moves that last only a few days. Rather, I am proposing to be nimble enough in one's economic and market analysis and investment decisions to adjust one's portfolio exposures as conditions dictate.

As investors have learned from the recent past, investing is more than merely allocating assets and then walking away to let time perform some sort of magic. Successful investing requires continual study and decisiveness. You don't have to be tuned to the market's every move all day long, but you should monitor a handful of key economic indicators so that you can be aware of shifts and undercurrents in time to react and preserve more of your hard-earned wealth. It is a discipline that cannot be underestimated and, as we all know, its reward is well worth the effort.

My purpose in writing this book is to explain the benefits of *tactical active asset management* and how this approach is a vitally important tool for today's investment professionals and their clientele. Throughout the book we will address active management and economics-based investing; the principles of economics-based investing; risk and reward and true diversification using ETFs to gain exposure to the broad market and specific sectors; and other topics. In addition, we are including our latest 2013 outlook, an in-depth look at what's happening in the economy, the markets, and all the factors that influence them. You will also find a calendar template to help you keep track of significant economic events and a glossary of economic terms.

My hope is that, by reading this book, you will come away with a working knowledge of how to put the pieces of the economic puzzle together, and how to turn economic analysis and opinion into informed decisions in the market. Along the way, you'll also gain a clearer understanding of matching risk tolerance and investment objectives through the sheer versatility of active management.

Chapter 1

UNDERSTANDING THE BASICS OF MACROECONOMICS-BASED INVESTING

At Astor, we employ an active management strategy using macroeconomic analysis, starting with interpretation of the current economic cycle. This is not without its challenges. Economic signals can be mixed, and the economy can grow or contract at different rates at different times. To meet these challenges we devote ourselves to macroeconomic analysis, using a variety of indicators—including our own, proprietary Astor Economic Index.

To start our discussion, let's review the basics of the four phases of the economic cycle and the characteristics of each.

- **Expansion** usually lasts the longest of all the economic stages and produces the greatest amount of wealth. This phase is marked by low unemployment and higher corporate profits, which usually lead to stock market rallies. In simplest terms, when more people are working, producing more things, and investing more money, the economy is expanding.

- **Peak** is the euphoria stage during which stock prices appreciate sharply and consumer spending surges. This is also when companies tend to overbuild, overbuy, and over-hire. Excesses build up that are not healthy for the economy in the long run.

- **Contraction** may be an unpleasant stage, but it is a very necessary one. As the economy slows down or slips into recession, businesses begin to shed the excesses that resulted from expansion and peak stages. Consumer spending and investment decrease. Companies lay off workers and stock prices decline. Contraction is the mirror opposite of expansion, simply it means fewer people working, less is being made, and declining investments.

- **Trough** is when the contraction hits bottom. Large numbers of workers are laid off and consumer spending declines. Although the economy is still contracting during the trough, companies that are leaner and more efficient start to make money again. Lower labor costs and higher worker productivity (the result of earlier layoffs) help boost corporate profits. This allows the economy to get healthy again and returns the cycle back to expansion.

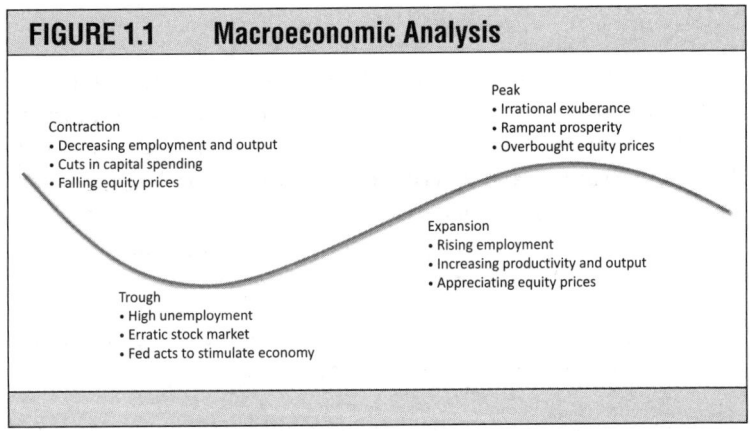

FIGURE 1.1   Macroeconomic Analysis

Peak
- Irrational exuberance
- Rampant prosperity
- Overbought equity prices

Contraction
- Decreasing employment and output
- Cuts in capital spending
- Falling equity prices

Expansion
- Rising employment
- Increasing productivity and output
- Appreciating equity prices

Trough
- High unemployment
- Erratic stock market
- Fed acts to stimulate economy

Defining the Business Cycle in Real Time

The business cycle is easiest to identify in the rearview mirror. With the passage of time, economists study not only the current economic data, but also the latest numbers in the context of previous data. That is why the National Bureau of Economic Research (NBER) makes its pronouncements after the fact, at the beginning and the end of a recession month.

From an active management standpoint, the challenge is determining how the economy is performing *right now*. Do the data indicate an expanding economy or a contracting one? Are the data mixed, indicating the next phase is not fully underway? Although there is a plethora of data by which to analyze the economy—from durable goods to vehicle sales to housing market statistics and reports from regional Federal Reserve banks—for our purposes here, we can break it down to the ABCs of economic analysis:

- Gross Domestic Product (GDP)

- Employment statistics

- Investment money flows and stock price momentum

Using this data, we determine if more people are working (as measured by employment statistics), making more products (as measured by GDP and other output statistics), and investing more money (as measured by money flows and stock price momentum, and following generic trend systems). If so, then the economy is expanding. Conversely, if fewer people are working, making fewer products, and investing less, then the economy is contracting.

GDP

Gross Domestic Product (GDP) is one of the most comprehensive measures of economic health, reflecting the physical output of businesses. GDP reflects the sum of consumption, investment, government spending, and exports, minus imports. Of these components, the largest is consumption, accounting for about two-thirds of the total. Little wonder then, that consumer spending is so closely watched. Even though GDP is a lagging indicator that is subject to revision, it is a vitally important gauge of the U.S. economy that is watched by everyone from the Federal Reserve Board of Governors to traders on the floor of the stock exchange. Granted, GDP does have some limitations. For example, it tends to understate the service and technology sectors, and it subtracts from U.S. output the goods and components imported into the U.S. by American multinationals from their overseas operations. Nonetheless, since those limitations are consistent quarter-to-quarter, GDP acts like an index, reflecting the relative strength or weakness of the economy.

You don't have to be an economist to decipher GDP or to understand what's happening in the economy. When a GDP report is released, the first questions to consider are:

- How is the economy performing compared to the previous quarter?

- How does the economy compare to a year ago?

- Is the GDP rate of growth increasing, which would indicate relative improvement in the economy?

- Or, is the rate of growth declining, which shows that economic growth has slowed?

Occasionally, GDP "goes negative," showing a quarterly growth rate such as -1.0 percent. Obviously, that doesn't mean industrial plants have kicked into reverse and are now "unmaking" goods. Rather, the rate of production has declined in the most recent period from the previous quarter. A negative GDP reading is a sure sign of a contracting economy. By classic definition, a recession occurs when there are two sequential negative GDP quarterly numbers. Increasing unemployment and declining stock prices, which can be just as painful as a classic recession, also characterize economic contractions.

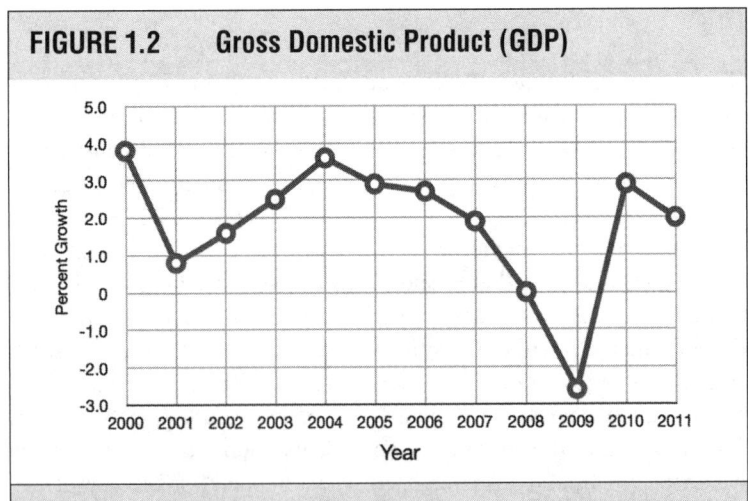

FIGURE 1.2   Gross Domestic Product (GDP)

Line graph shows fluctuations in GDP, from the strong economic growth of 2000 to the contraction during the 2008 to 2009 recession when GDP "went negative."

Another insight that can be gleaned from the GDP report is the level of inventories. Inventories are not part of the GDP equation since goods in the warehouse today were previously counted as output. However, the report does make note of inventory levels, which can influence the interpretation of the GDP number. For example, a strong GDP output number looks less rosy if growth in output resulted in higher inventories instead of increased consumer sales. Furthermore, when inventories decline because consumption has increased, it is a sign that economic activity may be picking up soon.

Employment

Employment has broad impact beyond the immediate economic implications. Who has a job, who does not, and who is still looking, are all important and emotional considerations for the economy. People who have lost their jobs or who are afraid of losing them are reluctant consumers and far less likely to commit to any big-ticket purchases. Jobless fears can also sour investor sentiment.

Employment is such an integral part of the economy that it is specifically mentioned by the Federal Reserve in its goals of monetary policy. In addition, employment is tied directly to the business cycle. In a contracting economy, growth in demand slows and inventories build. Companies cut back production and lay off workers. This helps companies reduce their labor costs, become more efficient, and improve profitability. During a recession, worker productivity (output per employee) typically improves. As the economy recovers and demand picks up, companies can benefit from lower labor costs for a limited time. Eventually, however, demand will reach the point at which production must be expanded and additional workers hired. Initially, productivity will decline. However, expansion in payroll signals that economic recovery is underway.

What's most significant about productivity after an economic contraction is the degree to which the benefits linger. For example, let's say a company has 100 workers making 100 widgets a day. When the economy contracts and demand slackens off, the company is forced to lay off workers. At first, there are 70 workers making 70 widgets a day, and then 50 workers making 60 widgets a day. This initial productivity increase is to be expected, but it's nothing to get excited about because output is still down. When demand picks up, the company may be able to produce 70 widgets with those 50 workers before it must start hiring again. If the company has truly improved productivity, it will be able to increase production at a faster rate than it must hire workers. For example, if production eventually goes up to 150 widgets produced by 100 workers, perhaps through more efficient manufacturing processes or better use of technology, that is a significant productivity improvement. Contractions are painful, but they can often result in better and healthier economic growth in the long run.

To decipher what's happening to the economy in terms of employment, attention is focused on the monthly Employment Situation Report (known unofficially as the unemployment report). When this report is released, the statistic that gets the most attention is the unemployment rate. The absolute statistic is not as important as the relative change from one month to the next, and over a longer period of time.

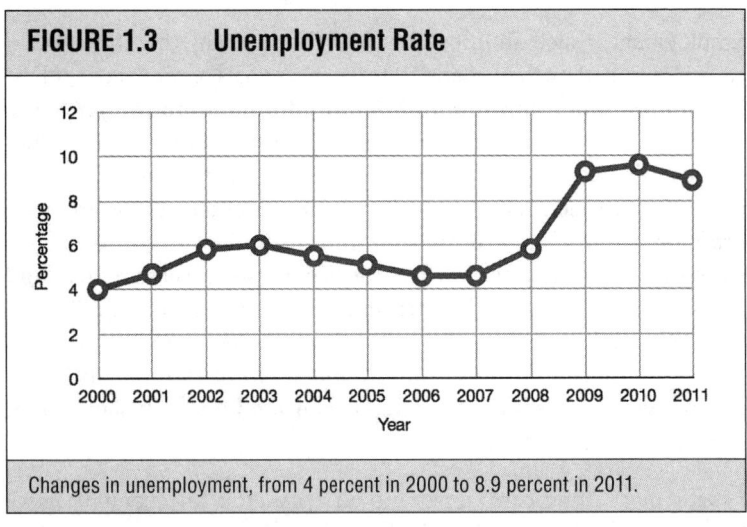

FIGURE 1.3   Unemployment Rate

Changes in unemployment, from 4 percent in 2000 to 8.9 percent in 2011.

The Employment Report is carefully tracked not only for what it reveals about the current labor market, but also for indications of how well or poorly the economy is performing. Increased joblessness, an increase in the number of newly unemployed persons, and a shrinking payroll number are all indications of poor or weakening economic conditions. Similarly, an uptick in job creation, a decrease in the number of newly unemployed people, and growth in the payroll number are signs of economic improvement. Keep in mind that the economy needs to add about one million jobs a year to keep growing, taking into account both new entries and people leaving the workforce.

Investment Money Flows and Stock Price Momentum

Investment money flows and stock price momentum reveal the underlying belief of how well the economy is performing. Typically, investor sentiment improves in step with economic growth and a better employment picture. The stock market, in fact, is one of the most important indicators of economic activity, reflecting the outlook for growth in corporate output as well as the profitability and the mood of investors.

When analyzing the stock market, we are not concerned at all about price-to-earnings (P/E) ratios. Although some analysts use P/E to suggest whether a stock is underpriced, fairly valued or overpriced, we don't put much credence in this ratio at all. Whether a stock is priced at $50 or $100 means little. The relative change in stock prices is what matters most, particularly when looking at the broader market. That's why we focus on the direction of money flows and stock price momentum.

It is far more important to know if additional investor money is going into equities and increasing the value of the stock market as reflected in the major indices such as the Dow, S&P 500, or the NASDAQ Composite. Or are investors pulling out of equities, causing stock prices to decline? In some instances, the stock market's behavior may be more telling than the economic data, particularly when the economy is perceived to be at or near a turning point in the trend—in other words at the peak or the trough.

When studying economic data or stock market performance, it is important to look beyond just a single report or a one-month time frame. Trends develop over time, and it often takes several months for a new trend to be identified and confirmed. With a longer-term perspective, the goal is to look for a consensus among the indicators, not only to confirm the trend, but also to gauge its strength.

FIGURE 1.4   Stock Market - Dow Jones Industrial Average

	Q1	Q2	Q3	Q4
2007	12,354.35	13,408.62	13,895.63	13,264.82
2008	12,262.89	11,350.01	10,850.66	8,776.39
2009	7,609.00	8,447.00	9,712.28	10,428.05
2010	10,856.63	9,774.02	10,788.05	11,577.51
2011	12,319.01	12,414.34	10,913.38	12,217.56

FIGURE 1.5   Impact of Economic Cycles

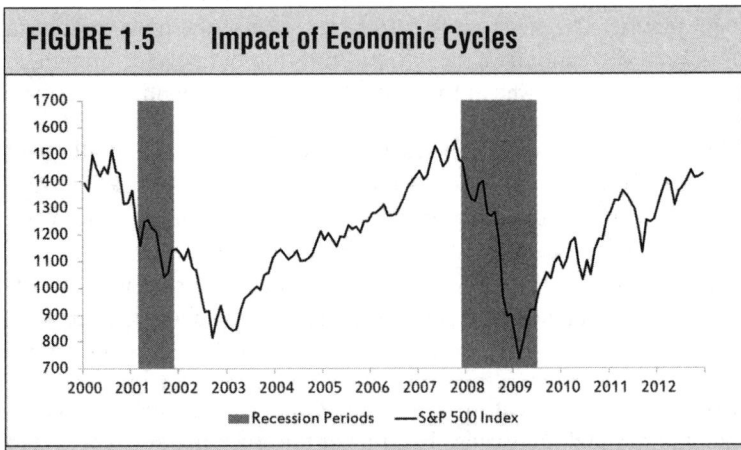

- Equity markets typically experience drawdowns during economic contractions and recessions.
- Identifying these economic periods can provide value by signaling when to shift allocations.
- Tactical portfolios have the flexibility to position into non-correlating assets.

Source: Bloomberg, NBER, Astor Calculations Data: 12/31/99-12/31/12

Participating in the Broad Market

Once the current business cycle is identified, an investment strategy can be put in place. Although these strategies have many variations, depending upon factors from the age of the investor to his risk tolerance, there are two basic investment concepts that should be followed.

1. An expanding economy is favorable to equity markets and therefore owning stocks.

2. A contracting economy is unfavorable for equities, and therefore stocks should be sold and/or short positions taken, and/or allocations to bonds and cash should be increased.

The best way to establish a long or short position in the equity market to capitalize on the current economic condition while using an active management strategy is with the broad indices. The indices allow investors to participate in the stock market's moves, both bullish and bearish. These indices, such as the S&P 500 and the NASDAQ 100, are better surrogates for the U.S. economy than any one particular stock.

That is not to say that stocks do not have a place in an investor's portfolio. Many investors buy stocks that they like or that they purchase because of potential growth in a particular sector of the economy. When it comes to active management, however, I believe the best way to capture the movements of the overall economy is with broad-based investment tools. Keep in mind that active management involves a portion of an investor's portfolio, and may account for 40 to 60 percent of an investor's equity holdings. Depending upon the portfolio mix, this may be as little as 20 or as much as 40 percent of the overall portfolio.

It is also important to realize that the primary determinant of a stock's movement is the underlying direction and momentum of the broader equity market. In fact, industry data show the market itself may account for nearly 80 percent of a stock's movement. Therefore, it is more efficient and effective for an investor to participate in the broad market through a stock index rather than an individual stock. An index, by definition, will reflect a large sector of the economy. This cannot be accomplished with any confidence by picking individual stocks. Even in a roaring bull market, there is always the chance that the one stock an investor picks is a laggard. Therefore, as we will discuss in Chapter 4, we believe the best way to achieve exposure to the broad market or specific sectors is with exchange-traded funds (ETFs).

THE ASTOR ECONOMIC INDEX: The variability in potential economic and market scenarios requires a solid, well-structured portfolio. A valuable tool we employ in our economic analysis and portfolio construction is the Astor Economic Index. This proprietary economic Index aggregates all the economic data we analyze into a single value. Portfolio beta is adjusted with equity allocations reduced or increased as the Index signals economic weakness or growth, respectively.

FIGURE 1.6   The Astor Economic Index

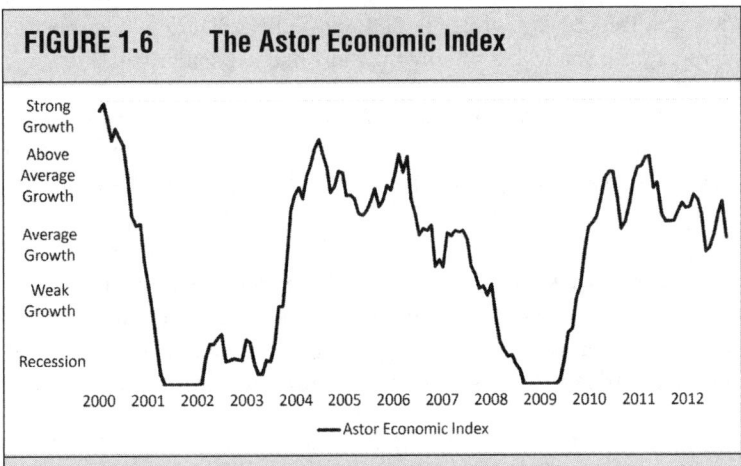

- Astor's proprietary economic indicator, The Astor Economic Index, aggregates the collection of economic data we analyze into a single value.

- The Index is the cornerstone of our portfolio construction process and creates a "road map" for equity exposure.

- Portfolio beta is adjusted when the Index fluctuates—equity allocations are reduced or increased as the Index signals economic weakness or growth.

Source: Astor Calculations

The Astor Economic Index provides a real-time "snapshot" of Astor's analysis of economic data in a single number, with values based on historical data. The Index acts as a kind of barometer for determining *beta* (or equity exposure) in the portfolio, reflecting the relative strength or weakness of the economic data.

The Index is based on Astor's analysis of economic data, GDP, employment, ISM, etc., with computer modeling developed by Astor's Director of Research John Eckstein. The value of the Index (and subsequent incremental increases or decreases in the Index) indicates the relative strength or weakness of the economy. As the Index moves higher or lower within positive (expansion) or negative (contraction) territory, we pursue the optimal beta for current economic conditions. Importantly, the Index helps Astor scale into and out of positions in order to increase or decrease beta. This is expected to smooth performance and increase agility in portfolio repositioning (as opposed to "stair-stepping" into positions when the economy is expanding or contracting). Furthermore, mistakes can be caught sooner, which has the ability to limit losses from unfavorable positions.

Pursuing Benefits in Any Cycle

Benefits can be achieved during all cycles on a risk-adjusted and/or outright performance basis. As an active manager, we believe it is essential to allocate part of one's portfolio to tactical asset management for the long haul. Challenging environments come and go, but when they appear it is sometimes difficult to ascertain. As you will read in Chapter 3, the market has behaved in distinctly different ways through specific cycles because of external factors, such as the increase in stock ownership among retail investors in the late 1980s and 1990s, or the period from 2008 through early 2012 when intervention-induced liquidity skewed how the market otherwise would have been expected to react to economic data. (The Federal Reserve, in effect, clipped the tails to minimize downsize risk, making the stock market perform like a utility stock. Had the central bankers not intervened to fight that uncertainty, maybe the outcome would have been better or worse; only time will tell.) Now we are in a new investment paradigm, uncertainty is going away and risk has re-entered—conditions that are more favorable to a tactical active management strategy.

At Astor, our years of experience show that one of the best ways to adjust portfolio allocation is by measuring economic cycles and interpreting the signals. This time-tested approach, we believe, will be important in order to be agile and flexible, making investment decisions based on economic reality.

Chapter 2

OUTLOOK 2013 — IT'S ALL ABOUT DEMAND

"Will demand pick up?" This is the big question for 2013.

The overarching economic issue since the financial crisis has been a lack of demand. Prior to the financial crisis, consumers borrowed too much, spent too much, consumed too much, and in general overdid it. Overconsumption occured for whatever reason, lenders, government policies and regulations, or just personal carelessness.

Now, post-crisis, we are dealing with the effects of a lack of demand. Contrary to what many believe, loan demand is weak and the velocity of money (how much money circulates through the system) is at the lower end of the spectrum (another reason why interest rates are so low). Moving forward, the demand picture is paramount to determining the direction of the economy—and the market—in 2013.

What happens to demand—whether it picks up and the economy accelerates or it declines and the economy slows down or even contracts—will have a more direct and potentially sustained impact on the market than we saw over the past few years. As we stated in the Introduction, central bank and government intervention intended to "manage" the market (clipping the tails, as it were) turned what would have been viewed as risk, quantifiable and, thus, able to be mitigated and managed into uncertainty. Now the "training wheels" are coming off as central bank and government intervention fades. As we've said, this is a good thing—risk that can be calculated is far better than uncertainty. However, where there is risk, there is also urgency to act. As we will discuss in our outlook for the year, if economic risks are detected—e.g., a slowdown in output or a dimmer employment picture—then investors need to brace themselves for the market to act as it normally does: in other words, economic downturns equal stock market corrections. This makes the case for tactical asset management all the stronger.

Before further exploring our outlook for 2013, it is helpful to recap the economic landscape for 2012 and put into perspective the events, forces, and other factors that will impact 2013.

2012 Recap

Looking back, 2012 was an interesting year, as much of the drama disguised the real economic picture. The presidential election, fiscal cliff, and recurring European financial crises that spread from country to country masked the actual underlying fundamentals, both good and bad.

More so than ever before, markets moved on interpretations of what *could* happen, rather than on the probabilities of what *would* happen. In other words, the general preoccupation was evaluating uncertainty rather than calculating risk, a phenomenon that has been more pronounced since the financial crisis of 2008. Markets are a good mechanism for pricing risk; uncertainty, however, is vague and uncertain. When faced with uncertainty, markets become volatile and follow irrational patterns. Risk, on the other hand, can be calculated and evaluated with better opportunities to create efficient portfolios.

In 2012, recovery continued—albeit anemic recovery, but recovery nonetheless. Inflation remained in check, and rates stayed low as promised. Housing prices recovered a bit, or at least stopped declining. Employment growth was steady, but below trend and the economy's potential. GDP was positive each of the four quarters of 2012, ending the year with +2 percent growth, and corporate profits gained again, reaching near-record levels.

Stock market performance overall was good, in fact, it was a bit high given the economic statistics. But this has more to do with the large decline in late summer 2011 and the response to the debt ceiling crisis, which had made the economic data and the market performance look and feel like a contraction. This set the stage for a challenging first few months of 2012. However, the market rebounded, with some of the gain in 2012 actually being carryover from what should have occurred in 2011 (if the markets at that time had not needed to recover from the debt ceiling crisis).

Government payrolls continued to shrink and the debt grew, but the deficit shrank, which helped ease that burden. Europe's financial issues remained offshore with the biggest hindrance being psychological. China, the perceived growth engine for the world, sputtered a bit in 2012. Emerging markets under-performed domestic equity indices, and with more risk.

The second half of 2012 was more in line with appropriate evaluation of risk and return, and with economic fundamentals. As we moved into October 2012 and focused on the presidential election, the pursuit of returns came with more risk, and President Obama's re-election left the market in a quandary about whether the looming fiscal cliff would be averted. The 11th hour agreement only skirted the issue and 2013 began with few answers and far more questions, much of which would be addressed in coming months.

Of particular note were the relatively tight range and the low level of volatility in 2012, less than what the media headlines and general perception might lead one to believe. We have not traded in this tight of a range since before the financial crisis, going back to 2007. Going forward, this is unlikely to be the case in 2013, as we expect volatility to increase, reflecting a more normal environment, in which markets that trade freely based on fundamentals carry a greater risk premium. To be clear, *we do not expect markets to be materially more risky in 2013; rather, they will exhibit more normal behavior.* In fact, markets will likely surprise on the upside, but with more volatility.

2013—Modest Growth with a Chance of Acceleration

The projection for 2013 is for overall positive growth. Most economists forecast real GDP growth in the U.S. at two percent for the year, a modest but positive target that has roughly a 50 percent likelihood of occurring. This will be enough, however, for the U.S. to lead the way in growth among all developed markets.

Projected growth is tempered by the effects of the fiscal cliff solution, which will likely curb economic expansion—perhaps by one percentage point—compared to what would have materialized had 2012 policies been carried forward into the New Year. We consider these expectations to be reasonable and consistent with continued mediocre, but positive payroll growth. Keep in mind that while private sector employers have added about 1.3 million jobs on a net basis since the beginning of 2009, the public sector has lost about 600,000. With state and local revenues stabilizing, the hope is that the public sector will not continue to lay off workers in 2013.

The demand outlook will likely improve as capital spending is expected to pick up. The corporate sector, with strong cash balances and record profits, has thus far made only small capital investments, and long-term investments are at historically low levels. Could it be that the last barrier, or should we say excuse, has passed? Political uncertainty and fiscal policies are perhaps not optimal, but at least visible. Although growth lags the long-term trend, many have become more comfortable with risk and the direction of the economy for the medium-term.

We will keep a close eye on PMI data during the first quarter of 2013 for signs of sustained improvement. In fact, the weak reading (-0.1 percent) for fourth quarter 2012 GDP will likely prove to be a head fake followed by acceleration in the first half of 2013. While this might not lead to a full-on, runaway expansion and bull market, it should be the first sustainable advance, such that if we do hit a speed bump the result likely will not be a complete giveback like many of the previous runs since the financial crisis.

Although, as of this writing in the beginning of 2013, the data indicate economic growth, that's not to say there aren't challenges out there. We do see a continued lack of confidence in the economy. Even if demand picks up in the first quarter of 2013, it might not be enough to support the economy from here. In addition to the negative GDP reading for the end of 2012 as mentioned above, the Philadelphia Fed report was disappointing and jobless claims hit an unusual uptick. Although this is not enough to sound the alarm as of yet, if the Astor Economic Index signals a shift, we will adjust the beta of the portfolio.

Whatever surfaces—strength or weakness—it will be *real*, and the market will react accordingly, without the benefit of a safety net of intervention to buffer the market's reaction. Don't expect a quick dip if the economic data indicate the presence of strengthening head-winds. The "close your eyes and ride it out because in a few weeks it won't matter" reaction will not work as it did post-economic crisis, from 2009 into 2012 when the typical downturn lasted about six weeks and the market didn't decline more than ten percent. During those days, tactical asset managers looked like heroes for about two weeks, and then numbskulls after that because the market largely ignored the fundamentals.

Although it was hard to identify at the time, in hindsight we can see that over the past five years, the market did a little more than bounce between highs and lows as the economy experienced no sustained expansion or contraction. Every time we got near the highs, the market dropped back, and when we explored previous lows, the market quickly rebounded. Timers loved this environment, but should financial success really be tied to when an investment is made? In fact, as we discuss in Chapter 3, tactical asset management should add more value to portfolio construction than timing or static portfolio construction.

As our analysis showed the period from 2009 to 2012 resembled the 1990s, when the market rebounded from any setbacks (fundamental or technical), as demand for stocks outweighed rational risk measures. The 2009 to 2012 period experienced a similar return profile, albeit for different reasons. Both periods were unsustainable and fundamentals ultimately prevailed. Following the run-up in stock valuations in 1999, fundamentals brought the market back down to rational levels. Today, fundamentals will likely regress to a more normal growth profile reflecting a sustained recovery and normal volatility. In other words, disappointing fundamentals should produce lower market prices and improving fundamentals should produce positive market performance. This is good news for market managers and for fundamental tactical managers.

Looking specifically at 2013, if there is a significant headwind in the form of economic data indicating a downturn or the return of fiscal drama, the result could be a real correction, potentially 20 to 25 percent and lasting two to four quarters. Just because the first market move without any intervention was up, don't be fooled that this will always be the case. Granted, we don't believe the economic data will decline as severely as in 2007 and 2008, but a slowing of output data and poor job growth shouldn't be shrugged off because we've been through far worse. Just because you've survived double pneumonia, don't think you can run a marathon with the flu. In the new market paradigm of visible risk, the market's reactions will be more typical—hence, the need to be vigilant and agile.

Allocating a portion of one's portfolio (depending upon individual risk tolerance, investment horizon, and the like) to active management, as you will read in upcoming chapters, may very well be a prudent move because of the ability to measure and manage risk and potentially avoid a drawdown. Remember, a 20 percent portfolio decline needs roughly a 40 percent increase to get back to break-even. When corrections last long enough and go deep enough, they will change how you reach your financial objectives.

With an active management approach, there are also opportunities to take on bigger positions with measurable risk. The risk of losing 15 percent, while not pleasurable, would certainly be viewed as preferable to the possibility of losing everything. Therefore, equities are favored when and where risk can be measured and mitigated, because risk is more likely to be rewarded when managed appropriately.

Bottom line—*wealth destruction seems to be off the table for 2013, but risk is real—and the need for alertness and agility underscore the importance of tactical asset management.*

Deflation and Inflation—No Big Worries for 2013

The biggest risk from a lack of demand is deflation. Deflation is not just lower prices, but a lack of increased demand at lower prices—a phenomenon we have seen in the housing market as lower prices did not spur more sales. Similarly, lower rates did not increase loan demand. The Federal Reserve utilized quantitative easing to head off a decline in demand, and it appears to have moved the needle. The jury is out on the cost to achieve the minor pickup in demand, but for the time being deflation is not a major concern.

We also do not see inflation as a significant issue. Inflation indices, CPI, PPI, and PCE, in 2012 were all below 1.9 percent (excluding food and energy), and the projection for inflation in 2013 is also below 2 percent. Given that unemployment remains above 7.5 percent, wages are flat, and capacity utilization rates are below 80 percent, we are not overly concerned about inflation in 2013.

The reason? The employment picture. The biggest catalyst for inflation is higher wages, without which it is difficult for the aggregate price of goods to increase.

In 2012, interest rates on the short end remained below GDP and inflation rates, reflecting the still-accommodative Federal Reserve. We believe the Fed will leave rates low until inflation perks up above 2.5 percent or unemployment falls below 6.5 percent. That being the case, we do not foresee runaway higher rates for 2013.

There is a fundamental relationship between short-term rates and GDP. Even the most pessimistic forecast of GDP is still well above the current two year rate, which means that a normal rate environment is higher than today's rate of a few basis points. That can cause stress on a fixed income portfolio, but hardly makes for a devastating event. In fact, during periods of low to high rates, equities will soften if not offset the principle erosion on the fixed income side.

Eye on the Fed

The Fed has a plan—the intention, stated a few years ago—to keep rates low for an extended period through 2015 or so. Since then, what were 10-year instruments have become 5-year instruments and soon will become short-term instruments, well before rising rates erode principle values. Duration risk reduces every day as equity valuations appreciate. If fixed income investors redeem treasuries when they mature and subsequently reinvest at the then-higher rates, research has shown that investors will receive a higher average rate by reinvesting short-term during a rising rate environment.

In early 2013, Fed minutes gave the first, faint signs of serious discussions about when to cease making monetary policy more accommodative. Careful reading of the minutes and the speeches of the governors makes it clear that the Fed is talking about when to *stop buying additional securities,* not about when to sell them or when to raise rates. To be clear, we do not expect any monetary policy tightening this year. What is possible is increased dissention on the Federal Open Market Committee (FOMC) over the prospect of further security purchases. It is also possible that the Fed may stop adding to its stock of purchased treasuries; in other words, cease QE3, perhaps toward the end of the year.

Signs from the FOMC potentially indicating the end of the massive asset purchases the Fed embarked on more than two years ago have put investors on notice. Even though the Fed has not come close to signaling a tightening campaign, investors have become concerned with high duration and sensitivity to the treasury market. Yields have maintained at historic lows for some time as economic risks have been continuously present.

Of course, this outlook for possible Fed action is subject to revision, based on the strength of the economy. We assume that inflation expectations remain well-anchored near the Fed's target. For now, it's a tiny cloud, far off in the blue sky, but eventually the day of tightening will arrive.

Looking back, 2012 was another good year for income funds and the fixed income markets. As we saw in equities, the first quarter of 2012 was responsible for the majority of the total returns. The last two quarters of 2012 looked to be more of an indication of what 2013 may have to offer as programs that focused on achieving yield outside of treasuries fared better.

Into the end of 2012, we began to observe a changing dynamic in higher yield levels across the treasury curve. If 2013 plays out in a positive fashion and we escape the first quarter relatively unscathed from looming fiscal issues, that picture may clarify further. The move in the yield curve is most likely toward steeping, especially as the beginning of tightening is still a ways off.

In the scenario described previously, risks are to higher duration and higher credit quality fixed income, which has been a safe haven and provided solid returns for investors for the better part of three years. The key component to this thesis is an uptick and further stabilization in the economy. Even as high yield has had a long run, and in the view of many we are in the late innings of this game, an initial interest rate inflection point should still bode well for this asset class as investors trade their risk aversion for riskier assets.

Meanwhile, the deficit and the debt ceiling continue to make headlines in Washington; nonetheless, it's important to keep this in economic perspective. Paying off the debt is not the issue as it's not the intention. Rather, service on the debt is the important statistic. Currently, that debt service is very low—less than two percent of GDP. In addition, the deficit is not as big as it has been in the past few years, and that is going to help the economy.

Another feature of 2012 was the initial sign that "identifiable risk" was returning, rather than unknown uncertainty. As we stated, sometime in the second quarter of 2012, central bankers took the training wheels off the system and stopped trying to guide (or manipulate) markets through every bit of uncertainty. After that, the first bit of "certainty" became "identifiable risk." Now, as we look forward, there are headwinds to economic growth—including those related to the fiscal cliff and its solutions. What does that mean? When conditions deteriorate or when one or a few large companies miss their earnings, asset or stock prices should decline. There will be components and sectors that have done very well in a protected environment that won't do as well, and there may even be some that won't (and shouldn't) be around any longer. The return of risk will expose all of that. For tactical managers that specialize in identifying those kinds of risks, this is very good news indeed.

Gold, Currencies, and Energy

With only a small likelihood of a fiscal crisis developing in 2013, gold will not benefit from the tailwind of being a safe haven. Nor will inflation be an issue, which otherwise could help gold. What drives gold is very short-term rates. Short-term rates are likely to rise at least to normalization, somewhere in the vicinity of GDP, and that will be the biggest challenge for gold. Therefore, we are not looking for 2013 to be a shining year for gold.

In fact, with stocks likely to approach or take out the all-time high this year or next, it will make it harder for investors to hang onto their gold. We foresee large holders of gold switching to stocks, continuing the recent correlation that we've seen between stocks and gold.

In currencies, we predict that the euro will survive; not much of a prediction as the actions of European Central Bank (ECB) President Mario Draghi and the ECB central bankers are clear, as are his goals. This will likely prevent a substantial dollar rally as the euro will find some footing. The big news in this sector will likely be a weakening yen against the euro, while the dollar slightly weakens (although not much on a net-to-net basis). A race to devalue will begin in 2013, but the winner will not be selected for years. Currency policy at times can be the root of financial market uncertainty, and this certainly could be the beginning of a currency war. But with weak global demand, it will take several years of currency moves to impact trade and investment flows.

Commodities, in general, have run their course, and we are not looking for 2013 to be a strong year for commodities.

Some interesting developments in oil have changed the supply and demand picture. In the recent past, the U.S. imported two-thirds of its energy. However, as any good economist will tell you, if the price of anything gets high enough, supply increases and demand decreases. That is exactly what has happened in energy. Supply has also been boosted by new technology that has improved efficiency in energy production, along with large discoveries of natural gas. Now, the U.S. produces two-thirds of its energy domestically.

As with anything in the economy, the oil supply and demand balance will probably overcorrect and drive prices down, which initially will be supportive of the economy and quietly help with pricing. With lower energy costs, consumers could translate that savings into higher spending elsewhere.

FIGURE 2.1 Economy Sector Performance

2000	2001	2002	2003	2004	2005	2006	2007	2008	2009	2010	2011	2012
Energy 76.36%	Consumer Discretionary 17.69%	Consumer Staples 1.02%	Technology 66.36%	Energy 34.77%	Energy 31.36%	Materials 34.69%	Energy 37.61%	Consumer Staples -25.91%	Technology 67.66%	Consumer Discretionary 27.66%	Consumer Staples 12.09%	Materials 21.70%
Healthcare 39.52%	Materials 9.95%	Materials -6.88%	Industrial 61.01%	Materials 24.77%	Healthcare 23.65%	Utilities 23.03%	Materials 33.99%	Healthcare -28.97%	Materials 57.92%	Energy 27.46%	Utilities 7.14%	Healthcare 20.69%
Consumer Staples 31.41%	Industrial 8.33%	Financial -8.65%	Materials 49.57%	Industrial 22.68%	Industrial 15.72%	Financial 13.65%	Healthcare 11.94%	Utilities -29.77%	Consumer Discretionary 56.54%	Materials 27.00%	Healthcare 5.83%	Financial 19.30%
Financial 31.25%	Financial 7.03%	Industrial -9.09%	Consumer Discretionary 41.46%	Financial 19.14%	Materials 13.46%	Consumer Discretionary 13.30%	Technology 11.50%	Financial -39.69%	Healthcare 51.55%	Technology 26.90%	Consumer Discretionary 0.73%	Consumer Discretionary 14.80%
Utilities 25.97%	Consumer Staples 1.97%	Consumer Discretionary -10.36%	Energy 38.05%	Utilities 16.47%	Technology 12.33%	Consumer Staples 11.02%	Utilities 5.02%	Consumer Discretionary -43.36%	Energy 47.35%	Industrial 24.91%	Industrial -6.41%	Industrial 14.53%
Industrial 5.90%	Healthcare -3.39%	Energy -10.82%	Healthcare 37.65%	Consumer Staples 16.35%	Utilities 11.29%	Technology 7.52%	Consumer Staples 4.77%	Materials -45.18%	Industrial 40.78%	Healthcare 19.38%	Energy -8.33%	Technology 8.96%
Materials 3.81%	Energy -6.25%	Healthcare -16.67%	Financial 34.90%	Healthcare 16.20%	Financial 7.30%	Industrial 5.89%	Industrial 2.87%	Industrial -46.17%	Financial 29.52%	Consumer Staples 18.43%	Financial -8.81%	Consumer Staples 6.46%
Consumer Discretionary -7.24%	Utilities -8.01%	Utilities -23.39%	Utilities 31.12%	Consumer Discretionary 14.67%	Consumer Staples 7.14%	Energy 5.88%	Consumer Discretionary -7.57%	Technology -47.73%	Consumer Staples 25.55%	Financial 17.23%	Materials -10.69%	Energy 3.05%
Technology -10.80%	Technology -13.57%	Technology -39.63%	Consumer Staples 17.05%	Technology 10.72%	Consumer Discretionary 0.11%	Healthcare 0.49%	Financial -17.34%	Energy -50.88%	Utilities 18.47%	Utilities 7.45%	Technology -11.48%	Utilities 0.77%

Legend: Healthcare · Consumer Staples · Technology · Materials · Financial · Energy · Utilities · Consumer Discretionary · Industrial

A comparison of sector performance, 2000 to 2012

Real Estate and Housing

Real estate looks promising this year with green shoots of recovery in the housing market, as home prices are trending upward. Recovery in housing, encouraged by real estate matrixes such as rent-to-valuations, will help support the economy. Forced savings and tax breaks have been making housing a good investment and an alternative to stocks and bonds—not rapid appreciation from financial engineering. Long-term housing statistics, however, are still somewhat lackluster.

The good news is that a solid foundation has been laid in housing. Think of it this way: People who bought homes over the last three or four years most likely got a decent deal, and the mortgages they obtained probably carry a decent rate. Banks during this time have also been more apt to be diligent in their lending practices, writing loans that are appropriate for individual income levels. Therefore, the housing activity over the past few years is not likely to cause problems going forward—these aren't the kind of transactions that one would regard as carrying a high risk of destroying the economy. Moreover, the suitability of these more recent transactions are generally supportive of the sector overall (and all the other houses out there). While we wish housing would be better, when viewed from the perspective of the health of recent transactions, we see it as a positive—and what might prove to be a hidden support beam for the economy.

Domestic Economic Sectors

Looking back, 2012 was a year of risk-on for domestic sectors with more speculative sectors such as financials (+23 percent) and consumer discretionary (+21 percent) outperforming the defensive sectors such as utilities (-1 percent) and consumer staples (+7 percent). We expect the risk-on environment to face significant headwinds initially from higher uncertainty regarding spending cuts and the debt ceiling debate.

Consumer discretionary, especially retail and durable goods, is expected to weaken from the impact of the expiry of the temporary two percentage point payroll tax holiday, higher income taxes for upper-income taxpayers, and uncertainty surrounding spending cuts. The consumer has held steady in recent periods, but a slowing in spending may be inevitable once the tax impact on incomes is realized.

The delay in the deadline for automatic spending cuts to March 1 may temporarily provide some upside to the healthcare sector, but that will be short-lived as the sequestration debate intensifies. Any spending cuts will mainly affect the healthcare providers, but will create secondary ripple effects on pharmaceutical and biotech, which fared well last year with growth of 32 percent.

The industrial sector outperformed the S&P 500 in 2012, even with investor concerns focused on the fiscal cliff and its potential impact on growth. With cautious optimism being shown toward the space, industrials have room to outperform in the coming year if we move beyond the fiscal cliff and outlook for growth begins to ratchet up. In recent years, the industrial sector has shown a propensity to outperform significantly when growth expectations are ratcheted up, such as in 2010. In more subdued economic environments, it has performed in line with or slightly under the broad markets. This type of risk/return could pay off in 2013, if growth expectations begin to move higher. If expectations for a pick-up in growth in the second half of 2013 are realized, the industrial sector is a good way to play an economic rebound.

The risk in this sector is if the headwinds for growth prevail and a global slowdown is prolonged. With three-plus years of slack in global growth and a continuous low interest rate environment, demand for manufacturing and infrastructure build-out supports exposure to this space. Fiscal restructuring could delay this, but should not prohibit it.

Export-dependent sectors—manufacturing (industrials) and to some extent chemicals (materials) and hardware (technology)—should benefit from a better growth picture for China in 2013 compared to 2012, with a consensus forecast of 8 percent growth, as discussed later in this chapter. There will be continued risk to sectors sensitive to foreign output, especially Europe. But the overall picture for 2013 looks rosy with the ISM manufacturing index and export index both trending positive of late and the ISM outlook survey of manufacturers indicating positive business sentiment.

As we look at equities, we must keep in mind what we stated earlier about the reality of risk in an economy in which there is no more safety net. If economic headwinds pick up, the impact on the market is likely to be more substantial than before, and if the economy improves, the market could really surprise on the upside. Those who have succeeded in the past by timing trading ranges are unlikely to experience an easy time in 2013 as the trends will be harder to hang onto. This is the kind of environment that tends to favor tactical asset management, and reward equities for appropriate risks taken.

Stock and Bond Correlations

Typically, when stocks go down, bonds go up; when stocks go up, bonds go down. The reason for this normal correlation is simple: low interest rates are good for companies, which can borrow more cheaply, whereas higher interest rates are the Fed's way of slowing down the economy. When stock and bond correlations are closer to -1, otherwise known as a risk-on, risk-off environment, such as we have seen post-financial crisis, it becomes tougher to diversify a portfolio because either it's all going up or it's all going down.

As of this writing in early 2013, correlations of stocks and bonds are reverting closer to +1, which is a more favorable scenario for managing a portfolio to produce better returns with lower risk. When stock and bond correlations are higher, this is typically an environment in which individual asset classes are moving independently.

For fundamental tactical asset managers such as Astor, macroeconomic models work best when asset correlations follow normal, historic patterns. Low correlation also helps promote portfolio diversification, with strong performance in one area offsetting a weaker performance or even a loss in another.

International Outlook

The Eurozone is expected to have another year of flat growth or even recession. The German election in fall 2013 will be in the spotlight, but for now the political situation in Europe seems to have stabilized as electorates in the periphery countries accept long periods of low growth as the price of continued Eurozone membership. Austerity policies, not only in the Eurozone periphery countries but also in Spain and Italy, have resulted in shrinking GDP and rising unemployment over the last 18 months. Although things are calmer at the moment, it is easy to imagine political developments that could return the Eurozone crisis to an acute phase.

Meanwhile, the United Kingdom also seems poised for another year of low but positive real GDP growth; it is forecasted to rise by about 1 percent. However, even the British government expects the current austerity phase to last until at least 2018.

In Japan, there have been some interesting developments following the election of Shinzo Abe as Prime Minister. His campaign was notable for an aggressive stance toward both China and the Bank of Japan (BOJ). We will assume that conflict with China is not in the cards, but what about the BOJ? As a candidate, Abe insisted that the BOJ has not done enough to lift Japan out of its 15-year deflation. He is pushing for 2 percent inflation; however, given that the bank has not been able to engineer 1 percent inflation, it is not clear how raising the target will change anything. Connected with the inflation target, Abe is also calling for unlimited quantitative easing. We expect the BOJ to pay lip-service to a new, more aggressive stance, but not to see much success in igniting inflation in 2013.

Among the developing markets, after some scares of slowing growth in 2012, more recent signs out of China are positive. As noted above, the consensus of economists is for growth in China of about 8 percent in 2013—better than 2012, but below the breakneck average pace of 9 to 10 percent enjoyed in the previous decade.

The other largest developing markets, Brazil and India, are likewise expected to grow more strongly in 2013 than they did in 2012, although below the pace of the last decade.

Conclusion: Slow and Steady

The overall expectation is for 2013 to be another year of growth below the long-term trend. In the U.S. we will face yet another major fiscal reckoning point, which will impact growth domestically to some degree, but will also have psychological ramifications globally. However, this year appears to have a different set up than we've seen recently.

Expectations are for growth to be low in the first half of the year, while the second half may see an acceleration in growth. This is the opposite of what we've seen the past two years as growth expectations improved into the first quarter, and then faded as the year continued. If our views for moderate but improving fundamentals are correct, that should support modestly higher risk taking. And visible risk, after all, is a positive—not a negative. With risk comes the ability to measure and mitigate—and potentially profit from it.

Chapter 3

THE CASE FOR TACTICAL ASSET MANAGEMENT

Here at Astor, our years of experience and research have proven that one of the best ways to adjust portfolio allocations is by measuring economic cycles, which are the fundamental backbone of the financial markets. Our strategy has been time-tested to succeed. Challenges will occur; the key is whether anything is learned after the challenge is over. Although we may see periods during which fundamentals are overridden by external factors, for example during the 1990s, it is more likely that fundamental signals will be valuable in the coming years, as they were over the last decade.

Astor is in its 14th year of managing client assets in our macro-based, actively managed strategies. Over the years, we have experienced and managed through multiple economic cycles. In the aftermath of the tech bubble back in 2002, we were able to achieve positive returns for our clients when the markets corrected with a near 50 percent decline. In 2008, we identified a challenging market and sidestepped much of the market's drawdown and wealth destruction for our clients. Subsequently, we participated in much of the market's 2009 to 2010 rebound. The years that followed have proven to be the most challenging from an active management standpoint.

Sovereign debt issues together with the U.S. fiscal cliff drama have certainly created a problematic backdrop to economic development.

An overlay of Federal Reserve-injected liquidity measures to promote demand and risk taking in a meager environment have posed challenges to economic analyses not seen before. Within this environment, we believe we have done well for our clients even though recent annual performance has lacked. Protecting wealth by reducing volatility and drawdown in a portfolio is—and has been—one of our main goals.

The experience of each of these cycles illustrates the benefit of real diversification—not merely spreading equity exposure around to different types of stocks and adding some fixed-income holdings, but rather to achieve *true asset diversification through active management.*

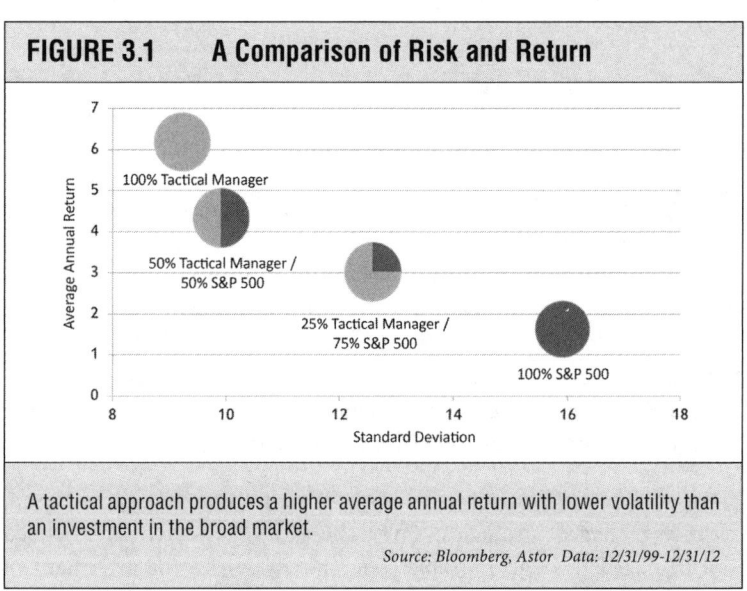

FIGURE 3.1   A Comparison of Risk and Return

A tactical approach produces a higher average annual return with lower volatility than an investment in the broad market.

Source: Bloomberg, Astor Data: 12/31/99-12/31/12

As we have stated, active management for Astor means using economic analysis to determine the most opportune times to buy and sell equities—namely, buying during economic expansions and selling (even short-selling) during economic contractions. We are able to accomplish this by utilizing investment instruments that represent a broad sector of the market. An effective way to accomplish this objective is with exchange-traded funds (ETFs), which can be used by money managers and individual investors alike to gain exposure to indices and sectors.

Given the dominance of equities in most investor portfolios these days, it is extremely important to recognize how active management can produce potentially significant returns that at least commensurate with the long-term, historical return associated with stocks of 12 to 15 percent over time. In this chapter we will look at tactical asset management—a dynamic approach based on specific criteria for when to buy and when to sell.

What Does Tactical Mean?

Historically, investors took a passive approach to investing, which meant portfolios often mirrored broad market indices and experienced little adjustment over time. Portfolio diversification meant a mix of stocks and bonds. However, as financial markets became more complex and intertwined, the market impact of geopolitical and economic events increased in magnitude. These events have caused a need for more robust and flexible investment styles to help clients achieve their investment goals. As the market environment changed, actively managed strategies like tactical asset allocation have provided value to investors. A tactical strategy allows managers to create dynamic portfolios by varying overall market exposure through changes in the weights of individual assets and asset classes. The main objective of these strategies is to limit drawdowns in adverse market environments while attempting to pick up excess return through investment selection. Both fundamental and technical indicators can provide signals for when and how much to shift portfolio allocations. It is the ability of these strategies to "de-risk" from broad market exposure by raising cash levels or investing in non-correlating assets and asset classes that generate added value.

Of great importance is how accurately a manager's indicators produce sell signals. A portfolio with a 25 percent loss would need a subsequent 50 percent gain to become whole again. A strategy that can remove all, or a portion, of that loss means subsequent gains are creating new wealth rather than replacing lost wealth. By looking back at recent decades, we can gain an understanding of where *tactical* best fits into investment decision making as shown in Figure 3.2.

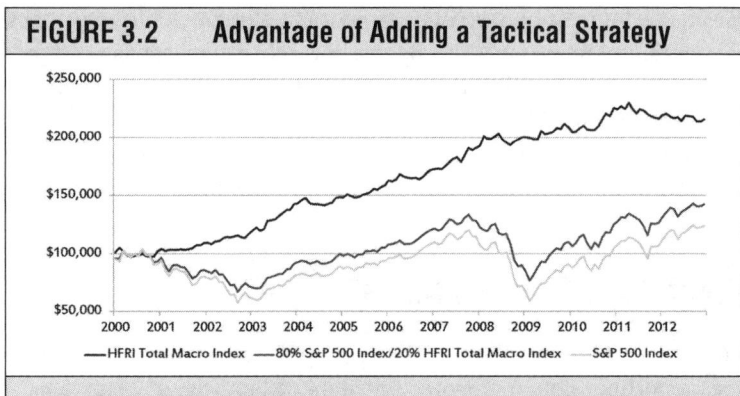

FIGURE 3.2 Advantage of Adding a Tactical Strategy

—HFRI Total Macro Index —80% S&P 500 Index/20% HFRI Total Macro Index —S&P 500 Index

- Allocating a portion of a portfolio to a tactical strategy can increase average annualized returns while lowering volatility, as shown by the middle line.

- Sidestepping a downward move in the market can help to build wealth sooner rather than just replacing lost wealth.

Source: Bloomberg Data: 12/31/99-12/31/12

Portfolio Allocation	Average Annual Return	Max Drawdown	Standard Deviation
100% S&P 500 Index	1.66%	(50.95%)	15.96%
100% HFRI Macro Index	6.08%	(7.32%)	5.46%
80% S&P 500 Index/20% HFRI Macro Index	2.75%	(42.45%)	12.99%

A Tale of Two Tapes

Over the last 25 years, we witnessed several market and economic environments. During these periods, investment strategies had varying levels of success due to the wide degree of value from certain indicators. We conducted an analysis of the periods 1988 to 1998 and 1999 to 2012 with a broad macro-perspective to evaluate these differences. For these periods, we captured the monthly returns of four separate data points: positive monthly momentum, negative monthly momentum, positive monthly fundamentals, and negative monthly fundamentals. These data points were determined by using a simple aggregate of economic data for fundamental signals, and a combination of moving averages and momentum indicators for technical signals. We compared the average returns of each of these points to the overall average return in all conditions in Figures 3.3 and 3.4.

FIGURE 3.3   Fundamental Signals

Average Monthly Returns of S&P 500 During a Weak and Strong Economy

Signal	1988-1998	1999-2012
Weak Economy	0.91%	-0.62%
Strong Economy	1.55%	0.74%
All	1.30%	0.15%

FIGURE 3.4   Technical Signals

Average Monthly Returns of S&P 500 During Periods of Negative and Positive Momentum

Signal	1988-1998	1999-2012
- Momentum	2.60%	-0.75%
+ Momentum	0.97%	0.39%
All	1.30%	0.15%

We note in the 1988 to 1998 period, all signals produced positive returns, including times of weak economy and negative momentum. In other words, a monthly sort by economics, momentum or random, all produced similar returns, and little extra value was added by identifying technical or fundamental strengths and weaknesses. The S&P 500 had a positive monthly return in nearly three-fourths of the months. Much of the over-performance and reduction in value to technical or fundamental analysis in this period was due to the substantial increase in the stock market participation rate, coupled with a long period of undervalued equity prices. Prior to 1990, less than one-third of the American public held stock, but by the end of the decade nearly half held stock as the internet, IRAs, and 401(k)s became widely available. (The 401(k) plan became popularized during the 1980s, and retail stock ownership rose through the 1990s, reaching a saturation point around 2000.)

Additionally, the Federal Reserve started to use monetary policy as a way to influence the stock market and thus communicate with the public. Even a 20 percent drawdown during the 1990 to 1991 recession did little to impact overall returns during the bull market of the '90s. A passive buy-and-hold strategy suited investors well during this period without requiring much thought or management.

In contrast, the 1999 to 2012 period showed substantial benefits from identifying strong and weak fundamentals and/or direction of momentum. The average monthly return of 0.15 percent meant that investors struggled to get returns in static portfolios. Value was added from sell signals generated by fundamental and technical indicators. Unlike previous periods, these signals were more effective as they actually coincided with negative market returns. Tactical managers took advantage of the opportunity this environment presented. Those who could allocate into defensive or neutral biased portfolios likely saw reduced drawdowns or even, potentially, gains in the volatile market cycles of this period. The continued influence of the Federal Reserve and global economic woes added to the period's volatility and at times put pressure on all types of strategies including buy-and-hold and tactical. Adding a tactical strategy to a portfolio during the two periods was positive; whether through increased returns, decreased drawdowns and volatility, or both.

The Impact of Tactical Strategies

Tactical strategies generally are not designed to replace an entire portfolio as they alone may not fulfill an investor's objectives. As a portion of an overall portfolio, however, these strategies proved to have merit during either of the two periods mentioned previously. Using a fundamental economic indicator as a proxy for a tactical strategy highlights the benefits. In Figures 3.5 and 3.6, we used The Astor Economic Index.

The Index, as explained in Chapter 1, provides signals on whether the economy is weak or strong through review of output and employment data points. Portfolio beta is then adjusted according to the level of the Index.

During the span from 1988 to 1998, most strategies produced positive returns. Buy-and-hold was the easy route and despite periodic drawdowns, a static allocation strategy provided the best results with little needed risk management. Figure 3.5 shows that adding a 20 percent allocation to a fundamental-based tactical strategy reduced risk and only marginally lowered returns. An investor in a tactical portfolio likely underperformed in this period as tactical sell signals added little value in a strong economic expansion and stock market.

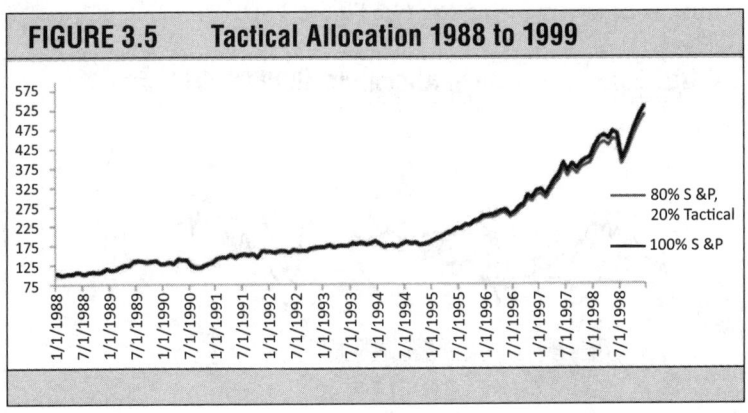

FIGURE 3.5   Tactical Allocation 1988 to 1999

Portfolio Allocation	Annual Return	Standard Deviation
80% S&P 500 Index/20% Tactical	16.00%	12.29%
100% S&P 500 Index	16.43%	13.14%

However, the environment was far different in 1999 to 2012, when large economic cycles, geopolitical events, and crumbling fiscal and economic conditions combined to create significant drawdowns and volatility. Investors who grew accustomed to buy-and-hold over the previous decade were now faced with a stressful market environment in which that strategy started to cause losses. The risk/return ratio moved significantly out of favor of investors. Wealth destruction continued as investors held onto static portfolios. On the flip side of the coin, investors with an allocation to tactical strategies were better able to navigate this challenging period. Average returns for the market were close to flat, but maneuvering opportunistically into and out of positions helped provide significant value to a portfolio. Unlike the prior period, adding the same 20 percent allocation to a portfolio mix increased the average return while also reducing risk (see Figure 3.6).

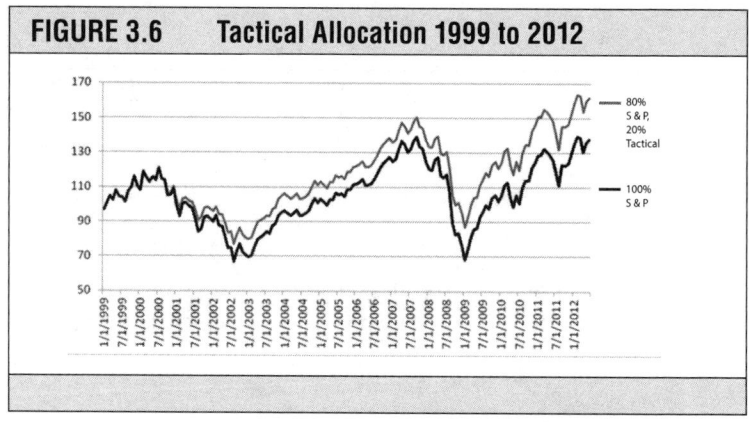

FIGURE 3.6   Tactical Allocation 1999 to 2012

Portfolio Allocation	Annual Return	Standard Deviation
80% S&P 500 Index/20% Tactical	3.63%	13.55%
100% S&P 500 Index	2.40%	15.99%

The Next Cycle

Tactical strategies have shown to provide value during all market cycles; however, they are typically most appreciated during adverse markets and economic contractions. As we move forward from the economic stresses of the past five years, we believe the foreseeable future will look something like a blend of the past. Risk and return profiles will also likely revert back to their mean values of the last 25 years. It is unlikely we will experience a parabolic rise in equity prices as seen in the 1988 to 1999 period; however, we are also unlikely to revisit the issues of the past decade having seen two +40 percent drawdowns within six years. Inside this range are numerous potential economic and market scenarios which will require a solid, well-structured portfolio to navigate the landscape. A tactical strategy will be a key tool. Benefits can be achieved during all cycles, on a risk adjusted basis and on outright performance.

As an active manager, we believe it is essential to allocate part of one's portfolio to tactical asset management for the long-haul. Challenging environments come and go, but when they appear it is sometimes difficult to ascertain. The uncertainty is why investing a piece of your portfolio in a tactical strategy is necessary.

Chapter 4

ETFS AND ACTIVE
MANAGEMENT IN ACTION

The instruments that can best help you to accomplish true diversification through bullish and bearish cycles are exchange-traded funds, or ETFs. An ETF is a collection of securities that tracks—or is intended to represent—the performance of either a broad or specific segment of the market. These instruments are a pure play on a specific index or sector. The transparency and low expenses of ETFs make them ideal investment choices for Astor's macroeconomic approach, to put our strategy into action.

Further, there is a vast range of ETFs available, covering multiple asset classes, sectors, and investment styles beyond the broad indexes such as the S&P 500, NASDAQ 100, and Dow Jones Industrial Average. Specialized ETFs allow us to gain exposure to a particular sector that is doing well and outpacing the growth of the overall economy. Whatever our investment hypothesis, there are ETFs that allow us to put ideas into action. Using ETFs, portfolios can be constructed that offer true diversification across various asset classes and in all types of market conditions.

Avoiding Catastrophe

At one time it was unfathomable, a well-established company that suddenly was trading for only a few dollars per share—or less. Consider Ford Motor Company that dropped below $2 per share in 2009, after trading around $30 in 2001. Or Bear Stearns, which in 2007 was trading above $150 a share and was sold in 2008 for $10 a share after the firm nearly failed. When Lehman Brothers went bankrupt in the fall of 2008, shareholders were wiped out. As these examples show, the risk of being in the wrong stock at the wrong time can be catastrophic. With ETFs, however, the risk of going to zero is nil. Yes, an ETF can see a downward move of 20 percent or more, but the chance of going to zero is remote, if not mathematically impossible. The reason is that ETFs are made up of dozens, and sometimes even hundreds, of stocks. Therefore, even if you have a few big losers in the index, the ETF will not go to zero. During the financial crisis, for example, a financial sector ETF was down 30 percent or so at one point, but was still a far better investment than the likes of Lehman Brothers or Bear Stearns. Granted, having an ETF lose a third of its value is painful, but it's not a complete washout.

The ETF Advantage

LOW COST: ETFs typically have low management fees and expense ratios because they require less active management than mutual funds. Most ETFs are designed to track a benchmark, which can mean fewer trades and lower portfolio turnover.

TAX EFFICIENCY: Since ETFs are passively managed, they usually realize fewer capital gains than actively managed funds. This reduces the frequency of tax gain distributions.

TRANSPARENT: ETFs provide investors with the required information to make informed investment decisions. Investors have access to all securities held within an ETF on a daily basis.

ALL-DAY ACCESS: ETFs trade throughout the day, enabling investors to lock in the market value of an ETF at any time during the trading day. Investors can enter or exit a position when they want, not just the end of the day, as with mutual funds.

VAST EXPOSURE: ETFs provide exposure to asset classes which, until recently, were off-limits to the average investor.

There are numerous ETFs, from those that track metals and other commodities to others that offer exposure to emerging markets or fixed income. There are even inverse ETFs that allow you to replicate a short position in a particular index. Buying inverse instruments, which go up in value when the underlying index goes down, allows you to hedge your portfolio. An investor could even construct a no-risk portfolio of longs and shorts using ETFs, with the security of knowing that positions could be liquidated at any time.

Praise for the ETF

I am on record as saying that the ETF is the greatest financial product innovation since the creation of the put! Allow me to explain. Back in the early days of options, there were only calls, which gave the buyer the right, but not the obligation, to take a long position in the underlying security. Calls worked great if you thought the market was going up, but if you wanted a short position you were basically out of luck. Writing calls would have given you short exposure, but with far too much risk exposure. With the creation of the put, it became possible to establish a short position by buying an option. When you buy a put, you have the opportunity, but not the obligation, to be short the market, and the only thing you stand to lose is the premium you paid.

ETFs, in my opinion, give investors the same flexibility: establishing long and short positions easily by buying an instrument—and without the complexity of shorting a stock. In addition, specialized ETFs allow investors to be long or short a particular sector or industry.

I prefer a long-term horizon and making investment decisions based on particular economic fundamentals. Plus, taking a sector approach avoids the risk of being invested in the wrong stock. Even if you correctly identify the market trend and pick a strong sector, you could still choose the wrong stock, whether it's one that lags because of a poor performing business unit or other fundamental problems. With an ETF, you gain sector exposure across multiple stocks. Using ETFs to invest, however, does mean that you won't get the sky-high returns of the rare stock whose gains outpace all other issues in a sector. But unless you are a professional stock analyst, your chance of accomplishing that is akin to finding a diamond on the beach. A far more prudent strategy is to use ETFs to gain exposure to the broad market and specific sectors.

Whether the overall trend is bullish or bearish, it is important to distinguish between the broad market and individual sectors. Even during 2008, when the stock market's performance was absolutely dismal, there were a few bright spots; among them, transportation. The lesson here is to look beyond your normal benchmarks such as the Dow when you are building a portfolio. Even if the entire market is down, that does not mean there will not be sectors that are performing well or that when the market rallies there will be sectors that outperform the rest.

Investing with ETFs allows you to think like an economist, instead of trying to be a stock picker. Your investment decisions are based on what you see happening in the economy and in particular sectors. This is a good approach no matter which way the wind blows in the future.

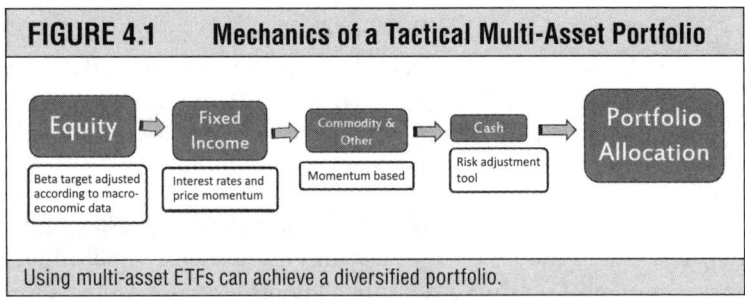

FIGURE 4.1   Mechanics of a Tactical Multi-Asset Portfolio

Using multi-asset ETFs can achieve a diversified portfolio.

Active Management: A Value Proposition

At Astor, our goal is to use true diversification to achieve less volatile long-term capital appreciation and lower drawdowns, thereby attempting to generate a more stable risk/return curve than our benchmark.

First, I want to emphasize that it is not the role of the asset manager, the professional who is actively managing a portfolio, to determine an individual's risk tolerance and market exposure. That decision is best made by the client, with input from his or her investment advisor, based on factors such as the investor's age, investment time horizon, earnings power, overall holdings, and risk tolerance. However, even if a client has no appetite for risk, as evidenced by large holdings in fixed-income assets, this individual may be a good candidate for a fixed income, active management strategy. If equities were a small percentage of the person's overall portfolio, then the active management portion of those holdings could be similarly confined to a small percentage.

If someone has a moderate risk tolerance, with roughly half of his or her portfolio in equities and half in fixed income, then at least half of the person's equity assets (or 25 percent of the overall portfolio) would be invested in an active management program. This approach significantly reduces the risk of the long-only equity approach of the portfolio during market downturns. Moreover, this approach also increases the potential return over time.

To illustrate this point, consider this scenario: An investor holds 100 percent of her portfolio in equities. If the market declines by 10 percent over time, the equity holdings would also be down about 10 percent, plus or minus a few percentage points, depending upon the performance of the individual stocks in the portfolio. However, if half of the portfolio were invested using an active management approach, then sometime during the market's decline, the investor would have at least exited the market. Or, if her risk tolerance allowed it, she would be short the market with half of her overall equity holdings. Thus, during the downturn, her losses would be at least cut in half compared to what they would be if she continued to hold her entire equity portfolio. With a short position, she could reap profits during a downturn that would offset losses on her equities, possibly to the extent that the portfolio broke even or made a small profit. In the worst-case scenario, the investor would have a smaller drawdown than with a full equity exposure and in the best case she would realize a modest profit.

Now, when the market turns and begins to recover, the investor can fully invest in equities again. But instead of having to make up for a 10 percent decline in her entire portfolio, she is starting off with a small loss, a break-even position, or a small profit. When the expanding market increases the value of the stocks in her portfolio, the investor reaps a larger return over time—and, more important, with reduced risk.

True asset diversification can maximize returns and minimize overall risk by taking advantage of opportunities presented in rising and falling markets. Most important, the strategies must be tailored to the individual's investment objectives and risk tolerance. In fact, that is the beauty of active management. When the optimal portion of a portfolio is committed to an active management strategy, an investor can protect against adverse market moves without putting too much of his or her holdings at risk. Active management is a powerful strategy that belongs in many investors' portfolios.

The key is for investors to work with their advisors to determine the right portfolio mix to match their risk profile, while pursuing their objectives for growth and capital preservation. Active management can be deployed to reduce risk and potentially improve returns and can be tailored to the investor. In fact, investment professionals who know their clients and their risk tolerance are the best to educate individuals about these strategies.

Over the long-term, the average annual return from owning stocks historically has been just under 10 percent. That is not a bad annual return if you can realize it, but most funds under perform their benchmark indexes on a regular basis. Moreover, even if you were able to achieve an average annual return of 10 percent or so, buy-and-hold has an inherent problem as a standalone strategy. On your way to achieving that target return, you could see your capital decline by 30 to 60 percent at times—and typically when you have the largest exposure to the markets. Further, as fate would have it, your portfolio could very well decline when you need your money most.

We are, by nature, emotional beings, and sitting through these stomach-churning market episodes is very difficult to do. In fact, most investors end up selling near the bottom and do not get back in until the market is well past the previous exit point on the way back up. With that action alone, you miss a significant portion of the market's return and need to work even harder to get it back. In other words, you have to sit through a 30 to 60 percent pullback only to achieve a long-term average return of less than 10 percent (if you did, indeed, sit through it). And, keep in mind that 10 percent is a simple arithmetic average return. Taking into account compounding, actual returns could be significantly less.

Some investors do hold through the ups and downs, attempting to weather the storm, because they have a longer time horizon for their financial needs. But what would happen if one of those financial needs occurred sooner than expected, or something came up and you needed money now? If that need arose in the middle or, worse yet, at the bottom of the drawdown (see years seven or eight in Figure 4.2), how devastating could that be? Aside from the financial need to make up a greater portion of those assets, it also reduces the capital base from which to compound your returns during the next positive period.

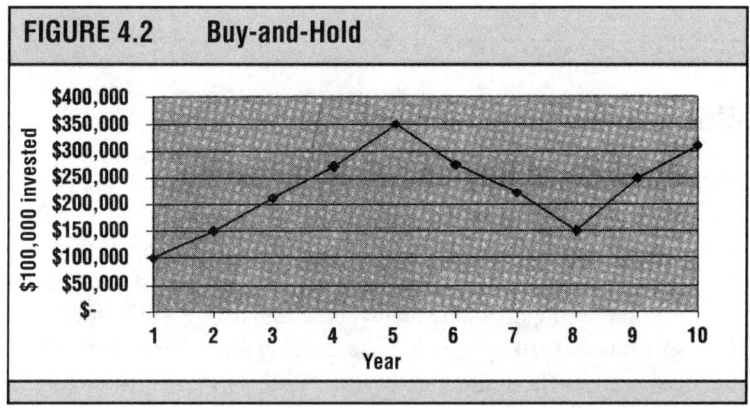

FIGURE 4.2   Buy-and-Hold

Active management, as discussed previously, has the potential to limit drawdowns without sacrificing upside potential, as illustrated in the hypothetical example shown in Figure 4.3. In this scenario, you would have a much easier time—and less worry—meeting financial demands in years seven and eight. The bottom line is that active management allows you to make financial decisions on your own terms, not the market's terms.

When the economy is doing well, you can make money by investing in almost any sector. But that is not where the real value of active management lies. When the economy is doing poorly, however, you can lose money in almost any sector. An active management strategy responds to changes in the economy and positions you to limit the losses. Now that is value!

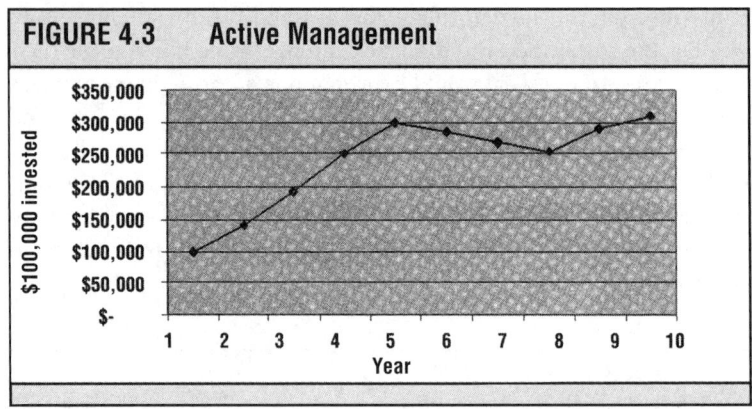

FIGURE 4.3   Active Management

Risk and Reward

The greater the risk investors are willing to take, the greater the potential reward they are going to require in return for that risk. Standard deviation is one measure of risk or volatility of a certain asset. (Treasury yields are labeled as risk-free assets because the risk of default or nonpayment on the coupon and principal is minimal.) Generally speaking, in order to reduce risk, you end up sacrificing return. However, active management has the unique ability to diminish overall risk without reducing long-term returns.

Why You Should Worry About Drawdowns

One of the most important considerations when choosing an investment is the amount of drawdown you will likely experience and how long it would take to recover.

- **Drawdown:** The total decrease (percentage or dollars) that your account falls from the highest peak value achieved in the account.

- **Recovery:** How long it takes from the low value in the drawdown to get back to new highs.

A key point to keep in mind is that the issue is not only lower draw-downs, which only require a smaller magnitude of return and a shorter amount of time to achieve break-even and then a gain. By controlling risk in the overall portfolio, you are better able to make more productive decisions with your other allocations. For example, if you control risk in 55 percent of your portfolio through active management, you could look at alternatives for a portion of the remainder—for example, 10 percent of the overall portfolio. That 10 percent could be devoted to alternative investments that, while riskier, have the potential to dynamically add value. You have more options to consider for that 10 percent portion because you have guarded against the potential drawdown of the overall portfolio through active management.

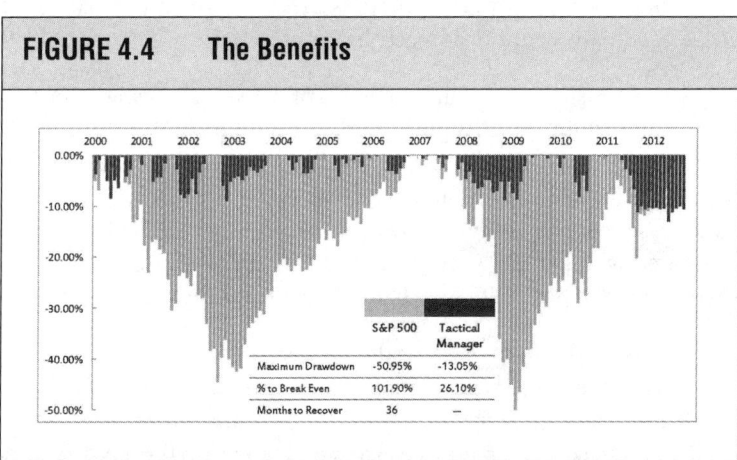

FIGURE 4.4   The Benefits

	S&P 500	Tactical Manager
Maximum Drawdown	-50.95%	-13.05%
% to Break Even	101.90%	26.10%
Months to Recover	36	—

- The broad investment universe and tactical allocation used in the portfolio have significantly lowered the drawdown compared to the broad market.
- In 2008, the portfolio experienced approximately 1/10th of the S&P 500's decline.
- Avoiding drawdowns provides an opportunity for wealth expansion rather than wealth replacement.

Source: Bloomberg, Astor Data: 12/31/1999 to 12/31/2012

The Case Study

Figure 4.5 depicts an all-equity buy-and-hold portfolio (the darker line on the chart) that correlated 100 percent with the S&P 500 for the time period shown. When the economic contraction and recession of 2008 to 2009 hit (the shaded area on the time line) the buy-and-hold portfolio suffered significant losses. Recovery from these losses will take a considerable amount of time and percentage gains. In contrast, the active management model (the lighter line) switches to a defensive position of fixed income-only during the contraction and recession, thus guarding against losses and positioning the portfolio for growth when the economy begins expanding again. The active management portion also includes a hypothetical higher-risk investment in 2010 to 2011 that could potentially result in a larger than average return.

As Figure 4.5 shows, the major benefit of active management occurs during uncertain or changing market conditions. With a significant reduction in volatility in the value of your assets, you can feel more comfortable making important financial decisions, and have a larger asset base to compound during positive market environments. Moreover, to reiterate, when overall portfolio risk can be contained, there is more opportunity to explore investment alternatives.

The points made in the case study are clear in Figure 4.6. The addition of active management created a much more desirable effect in the long term. Through active management, the portfolio drawdown was smaller, the recovery time was shorter, and, as a result, overall returns were greater with much less risk.

FIGURE 4.5   All Equity Buy-and-Hold vs. Active Management

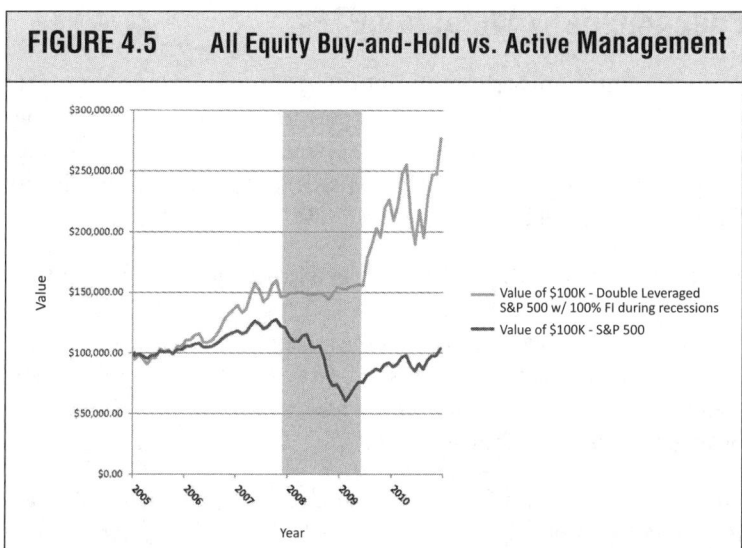

Comparison of buy-and-hold/equity-only with an active management model, which switches to a 100 percent fixed income position during economic contractions or recession.

Figure 4.6   Less Losses

	Buy-And-Hold	Active Mix
Beginning investment	$100,000.00	$100,000.00
Lowest value of account during period	$81,908.26	$98,022.68
Largest yearly return during period	9.63%	10.05%
Current Value (2010)	$117,052.30	$142,002.96
Out-performance of buy-and-hold by mix		21.32%

Comparison of buy-and-hold portfolio with the active management model mix. Although the active mix does post a larger yearly return during the period 2000 to 2010, the more important data point is the lowest value of the account during the period. Active management lost less than $2,000, while the buy-and-hold portfolio declined by more than $18,000.

Fundamentally Weighted ETFs

As the ETF universe has continued to expand, one of the developments that appears to have merit is the fundamentally weighted ETF. Among the newest entrants in these quantitative ETFs (along with offerings such as the Wisdom Tree's fundamentally weighted ETFs and Power Shares Intellidex ETFs) are the AlphaDEX® from First Trust.

We see the AlphaDEX® as being a particularly good fit for a fundamentally based strategy such as ours. The appeal of these products for fundamental managers is that they use fundamentals, not necessarily technicals or momentum, to select stocks that make up the index. Generally their out-performance correlates to Astor's signals on the business cycles—a definite win-win.

For example, when our fundamental analysis suggests a particular sector should be over weighted, buying the AlphaDEX® ETF for that sector provides additional overweighting. Therefore, we see these ETFs as good tools for implementing a tactical asset management strategy. The Astor S.T.A.R.—Sector Tactical Asset Rotation—program, for example, utilizes the AlphaDEX® ETFs to pursue its objective of investing in strong sectors and assets that have the potential to outperform broader market indices, regardless of the cyclical nature of markets.

Summary: Strategies for Tomorrow's Markets

Market corrections of the past have taught us an important, albeit painful lesson, one that we at Astor have been teaching clients for years. Rather than putting their hopes—and money—on buy-and-hold, investors must recognize the need to take a more active approach to investing. To meet the needs of these sophisticated investors, investment professionals should offer more than just the mutual fund flavor of the month or hot stock pick. Savvy investors are looking for strategies that will serve them not only in today's market conditions, but tomorrow's as well.

To meet the needs of their clients, investment professionals must understand the advantages of active management, which allows investment decisions to be made based on specific market conditions and other criteria, such as Astor's philosophy of macroeconomics-based active management.

Through active management, investors have the potential to improve returns and reduce risk. Moreover, they can bring true diversification to their portfolios to guard against downturns and improve returns in favorable conditions. This is vitally important in today's new investment climate with normalized risk patterns. As risk re-enters the investment picture (risk, as we've stated, is not a dirty word), it is best left to professionals who can manage it using a tactical approach.

Bullish or bearish, economic expansion or contraction, the cycles will continue. Savvy investors and the investment professionals who advise them should not be afraid when the cycles change. Through active management, they will be empowered to make bolder decisions which, over time, can improve returns while reducing unfavorable market exposure.

ABOUT THE AUTHOR

▲ ▲ ▲ ▲ ▲ ▲

Robert Stein is Senior Managing Director for Astor Asset Management and serves as Senior Portfolio Manager of Astor's mutual funds and separately managed account programs. Rob started his career in 1983 as a project analyst for the Federal Reserve under the chairmanship of Paul Volcker. He then held senior trading or portfolio management positions with Bank of America New York, Harris Bank Chicago, and Continental Bank Chicago, which was acquired by Bank of America. In 1991, Rob became the Managing Director of Proprietary Trading at Barclay's Bank PLC, New York. Returning to Chicago in 1994, he formed Astor Financial Inc. and later established Astor Asset Management, which provides investment advisory services to clients.

Rob is also the author of The Bull Inside the Bear: Finding New Investment Opportunities in Today's Fast-Changing Economy and Inside Greenspan's Briefcase: Investment Strategies for Profiting from Reports and Data. He is regularly featured in print and broadcast media for the financial world, including the Wall Street Journal, Bloomberg BusinessWeek, Investor's Business Daily, ABC, FOX News, Bloomberg, and CNBC.

Rob is the founder and president of the Dream of Jeanne Foundation and is the vice chairman of the board of trustees of Glenkirk, both of which help mentally challenged people participate in community life. Rob graduated from the University of Michigan and holds Series 3, 7, and 65 licenses.

Other Members of the Astor Asset Management Team

Bryan Novak joined Astor in 2002 and currently serves as Director of Trading. Bryan has been involved in the research and development of the trading and investment strategies at the firm. He was instrumental in the launch of the firm's mutual fund in 2009 and has served as part of the portfolio management team since 2004. Prior to Astor, Bryan was a trader for Second City Trading, LLC. He has experience trading in securities markets including equities, equity derivatives, futures and commodity markets, as well as pre-public equity investment structures. Bryan earned his Bachelor of Science in Financial Management from the Ohio State University. Bryan is a Level 1 CAIA candidate.

John Eckstein joined Astor as Director of Research in 2011. He serves on the firm's investment committee and is responsible for international global macro strategies. In 1995, John founded Cornerstone Quantitative Investment Group, a global macro hedge fund with peak assets of $600 million. At Cornerstone, he was responsible for all aspects of the firm's operations including fixed income, currency, commodity, and equity portfolios. Prior to Cornerstone, John was a researcher for Luck Trading Company, a commodity trading adviser. He is a co-author of Commodity Investing (John Wiley & Sons, 2008) and is a frequent speaker at industry events. He holds a Bachelor of Science from Brown University and a Masters in Public Administration (International Economic Policy) from Columbia University.

GLOSSARY OF ECONOMIC TERMS

▲ ▲ ▲ ▲ ▲ ▲

There are a variety of indicators that reflect at least one aspect of the U.S. economy. Some of the indicators are broad measurements, such as Gross Domestic Product (GDP), which gauges the output of U.S. business. Others, such as Vehicle Sales, have a far more limited scope. Taken together, these indicators provide in-depth information about how the economy has been performing and a hint of what is likely to come.

At Astor Asset Management, our economics-based approach to active management requires that we closely monitor economic data. While we give more weight to some indicators (such as GDP and the Employment Situation) over others, each report offers some insight. The best way to make informed investment decisions is with a thorough understanding of the current state of the economy (expansion, peak, contraction, or trough) and the strength or weakness of that prevailing trend. We also believe that investment professionals and their savvy clientele should be familiar with economic reports and indicators, to understand their meaning and discern their relative importance.

Following is a glossary of economic reports, with a brief description of each.

Agricultural Prices

Released at the end of each month

This report from the U.S. Department of Agriculture includes the prices received by farmers for crops, livestock, and livestock products. Data are derived from surveys of mills and elevators (grain); packers, stockyards, auctions, dealers, and other sources (livestock); and sample surveys and market check data (fruits and vegetable prices).

Beige Book

Released eight times per year

Commonly known as the Beige Book, the Federal Reserve's "Summary of Commentary on Current Economic Conditions" is published eight times a year. Each Federal Reserve Bank gathers anecdotal information on current economic conditions in its district through reports from bank and branch directors and interviews with key business people, economists, market experts, and other sources. The Beige Book summarizes this information by district and sector. The Beige Book does not represent the views of the Federal Reserve Board or the Federal Reserve Banks, but summarizes comments from businesses and contacts outside of the Federal Reserve System.

Business Inventories

Released the middle of each month

This report from the Bureau of Census includes three components. Monthly Retail Trade presents data on dollar-value of retail sales and sales for selected establishment, as well as a sub-sample of firms providing data on end-of-month inventories. Monthly Wholesale Trade includes data on dollar values of merchant wholesalers' sales and end-of-month inventories. Manufacturers report current production levels and future production commitments, as well as the value of shipments, new orders net of cancellations, month-end total inventory, materials and supplies, work-in-process, and finished goods inventories.

Chain Store Sales

(see ICSC-Goldman Sachs Chain Store Sales Trends)

Challenger Report

Released during the first week of each month

The Challenger Report is a monthly job outlook report from outplacement firm Challenger, Gray & Christmas.

Chicago Fed National Activity Index

Released at the end of each month

The Chicago Fed National Activity Index, released monthly by the Chicago Federal Reserve Board, is a coincident indicator of broad economic activity. An index reading of "zero" indicates that the economy is growing at its long-run potential growth rate. A value above zero indicates that the economy is growing above potential, while a negative value indicates that the economy is growing below potential. The index is a weighted average of 85 indicators of national economic activity. These indicators are drawn from five broad categories of data: (1) production and income; (2) employment, unemployment, and hours worked; (3) personal consumption and housing; (4) manufacturing and trade sales; (5) inventories and orders.

Chicago Purchasing Managers Chicago Business Barometer

Released on the last business day of each month

This report provides a regional view of the national economy, summarizing current business activity. The report is also known as the Chicago Purchasing Manager Index or Chicago PMI.

Conference Board Consumer Confidence Index

Released at the end of each month

The Conference Board Consumer Confidence Index measures the level of confidence that individual households have in the performance of the economy. Survey questionnaires are mailed to a nationwide representative sample of households, which are asked five questions to rate the current business conditions in the household's area: business conditions six months into the future, job availability in the area, job availability in six months, and family income in six months. Responses are seasonally adjusted. An index is constructed for each response and then a composite index is fashioned based on the responses. Two other indices—one to assess the present situation and one for expectations about the future—are also constructed. Expectations account for 60 percent of the index, while the current situation is responsible for the remaining 40 percent.

Conference Board Employment Trends Index
Released on the Monday following the Friday release of the Employment Situation Report

The Employment Trends Index combines eight labor-market indicators. This index includes: percentage of respondents who report jobs are hard to get; initial claims for unemployment insurance; percentage of firms with positions they are unable to fill now; number of employees hired by temporary help industry; workers with part-time jobs due to economic reasons; job openings; industrial production; and manufacturing and trade sales.

Conference Board Help Wanted OnLine Data Series
Released at the end of each month

The Conference Board **HELP WANTED ONLINE** Data Series measures the number of new, first-time online jobs and jobs re posted from the previous month on more than 1,200 major Internet job sites and smaller job sites that serve niche markets and smaller geographic areas. The new online series is not a direct measure of job vacancies. The level of ads in print and online can change for reasons not related to overall job demand.

Conference Board Leading Economic Index

Released mid-month each month

This index is designed to signal peaks and troughs in the business cycle. The leading, coincident, and lagging economic indexes are essentially composite averages of several individual leading, coincident, or lagging indicators. They are constructed to summarize and reveal common turning point patterns in economic data in a clearer and more convincing manner than any individual component—primarily because they smooth out some of the volatility of individual components.

Conference Board Measure of CEO Confidence

Released quarterly, during the first week after each quarter closes

The Conference Board Measure of CEO Confidence assesses CEO views of economic conditions. The report includes assessments of current conditions as well as the outlook for improvement and/or decline.

Construction Spending

Released on the first day of each month

Construction Spending, from the Bureau of Census, reports the dollar value of newly completed structures. Individual data series are available for several residential building types; nonresidential private building types; public buildings, and other public and private structures, such as roads and utility lines. Both current dollar and inflation-adjusted estimates are available. This release is used directly to estimate the investment in the structures component of the expenditures estimate of GDP. Since a building is not recorded in the data series until it is completed, this series is a lagging indicator of construction activity.

Consumer Confidence Survey

(See Conference Board's Consumer Confidence Survey)

Consumer Credit

Released on the fifth business day of each month

Consumer Credit, from the Federal Reserve Board, represents loans for households for financing consumer purchases of goods and services and for refinancing existing consumer debt. Secured and unsecured loans are included except those secured with real estate (mortgages, home equity loans and lines, etc). Securitized consumer loans, loans made by finance companies, banks, and retailers that are sold as securities are included. The two categories of consumer credit are revolving and non-revolving debt. Revolving debt covers credit card use whether for purchases or for cash advances, store charge accounts, and check credit plans that allow overdrafts up to certain amounts on personal accounts.

Consumer Price Index (CPI)

Released on the fifteenth of each month

The Consumer Price Index (CPI) is a measure of the average change over time in the prices paid by urban consumers for a fixed market basket of consumer goods and services. The CPI report, released by the Bureau of Labor Statistics, provides a way for consumers to compare what the market basket of goods and services costs this month with what the same market basket cost a month or a year ago. The CPI reports price changes in over 200 categories, arranged into eight major groups. The CPI includes various user fees such as water and sewerage charges, auto registration fees, vehicle tolls, and so forth. Taxes that are directly associated with the prices of specific goods and services (such as sales and excise taxes) are also included.

Consumer Sentiment Survey

(See Thomson Reuters/University of Michigan Survey of Consumers)

Current Account Deficit Report

Released quarterly, mid-month

The Current Account report from the Bureau of Economic Analysis reflects the movement of non-capital items in the balance of payments account. The report breaks out the balance on goods, services, and income. Changes in the current account balance are a useful barometer for the state of U.S. foreign trade as well as the flow of investment to and from the United States. A widening deficit on the current account is typical when the United States is purchasing excessive imports. The current account also provides a good measure of the performance of the United States in the international markets.

Durable Goods

Released at the end of each month

Durable Goods from the Bureau of the Census is the advance release of overall factory orders and shipments. Durable goods are industrial products with an expected life of one year or more. They include intermediate goods, such as steel, lumber, and electronic components; finished industrial machinery and equipment; and finished consumer durable goods, such as furniture, autos, and TVs. Data are reported for seven different industry groupings, plus the total. New orders are the dollar volume of orders for new products received by domestic manufacturers from any source, domestic or foreign.

ECRI Weekly Leading Index

Released each Friday

The Economic Cycle Research Institute's (ECRI) Weekly Leading Index is a weighted average of seven key economic data designed to predict economic conditions in the near term. Meant to be clearly cyclical, the index is designed to turn down before a recession and turn up before an expansion.

Employment Cost Index

Released quarterly on the last Thursday of the reporting month

The Employment Cost Index (ECI) from the Bureau of Labor Statistics is based on a survey of employer payrolls. The index measures the change in the cost of labor, free from the influence of employment shifts among occupations and industries.

Employment Situation

Released on the first Friday of each month

Payroll figures are reported each month by the Bureau of Labor Statistics in its Employment Situation Report. Payroll employment is a measure of the number of jobs in more than 500 industries, except for farming, in all states and 255 metropolitan areas. The employment estimates are based on a survey of larger businesses. The report also provides information on average weekly hours worked and average hourly earnings, which are important indicators of the tightness of labor markets. An index of aggregate weekly hours worked is also included in the release, which gives an important early indication of production before the quarterly GDP numbers come out.

Existing Home Sales

Released around the twenty-fifth of each month

Each month the National Association of Realtors (NAR) Research Division receives data on existing single-family home sales from over 650 boards and associations of realtors and multiple listing systems across the country. This data is included in the Existing Home Sales Report.

Factory Orders

Released during the first week of each month

The Factory Orders report from the Bureau of the Census includes the dollar volume of new orders, shipments, unfilled orders, and inventories reported by domestic manufacturers. Data are reported for numerous industry groupings, plus the total and specialized aggregates. New orders are a good measure of demand for each industry and in aggregate, and shipments are a good measure of supply. Unfilled orders are the backlog of orders that have been received by domestic manufacturers, but not yet shipped. Unfilled orders are one indication of the balance between demand and supply, most often used to indicate an excess of demand relative to supply.

Federal Open Market Committee (FOMC) Meeting

Meets eight times per year

The Federal Open Market Committee of the Federal Reserve Board (FOMC) meets approximately every six weeks to consider whether any changes need to be made to monetary policy. The FOMC is comprised of the seven Federal Reserve Board members, including the current chairman, and five Federal Reserve District Bank presidents.

FOMC Minutes

Minutes of regularly scheduled meetings are released three weeks after the date of the FOMC meeting

The Federal Open Market Committee (FOMC) holds eight regularly scheduled meetings during the year and other meetings as needed.

Gross Domestic Product (GDP)

Released on the last Friday of each month

Gross Domestic Product (GDP) is a measure of the total production and consumption of goods and services in the United States. The report, released by the Bureau of Economic Analysis, includes two complementary measures of GDP, one based on income and one based on expenditures. GDP is measured one way by adding up the labor, capital, and tax costs of producing the output. On the consumption side, GDP is measured by adding up expenditures by households, businesses, government, and net foreign purchases. Theoretically, these two measures should be equal. However, due to problems collecting the data, there is often a discrepancy between the two measures. The GDP price deflator is used to convert output measured at current prices into constant-dollar GDP.

ICSC-Goldman Sachs (ICSC-GS) Chain-Store Sales Index

Released each Tuesday

The index measures nominal same-store or comparable-store sales excluding restaurant and vehicle demand. The weekly index statistically represents industry sales. The standard period used for the index is Sunday through Saturday. The weekly sales index is presented on an adjusted basis to account for normal seasonality and to counter other data anomalies.

Import and Export Prices

Released mid-month each month

Every month, the Bureau of Labor Statistics collects net transaction prices for more than 20,000 products from over 6,000 companies and secondary sources to formulate the Import and Export Prices report. The overall import price index measures the price change of products purchased from other countries by U.S. residents. The overall export price index measures the change in the prices of domestically produced U.S. goods shipped to other countries.

Industrial Production/Capacity Utilization

Released around the fifteenth of each month

The Industrial Production index, released by the Federal Reserve Board, measures the change in output in U.S. manufacturing, mining, and electric and gas utilities. Output refers to the physical quantity of items produced. The index covers the production of goods and power for domestic sales in the United States and for export. It excludes production in the agriculture, construction, transportation, communication, trade, finance, and service industries; government output, and imports. Each component is weighted according to its relative importance in the base period. The report also includes Capacity Utilization, which gauges how much available capacity exists. The greater the capacity utilization, the higher the production level, which could indicate inflation (typically a measurement over 85 percent). Conversely, a low capacity number indicates economic weakness as industries are producing below their potential.

International Trade

Released around the ninth to the thirteenth of each month

The International Trade report from the Department of Commerce reflects the balance of trade, or the difference between exports and imports of goods and services. Merchandise data are provided for U.S. total foreign trade with all nations, with detail for trade with particular nations and regions of the world, as well as for individual commodities. Using the report, the importance of one country's economy may be analyzed in terms of U.S. trade. The report can further reveal to what extent overseas growth is contributing to the U.S. economic performance.

ISM Report

(See Manufacturing ISM Report on Business)

ISM Non-Manufacturing Index

(See Non-Manufacturing ISM Report on Business)

Jobless Claims

(See Unemployment Insurance Weekly Claims Report)

Job Opening and Labor Turnover

Released around the tenth of each month

The Job Openings and Labor Turnover Survey (JOLTS) is released by the Bureau of Labor Statistics (BLS). Data in the survey are collected and compiled monthly from a sample of business establishments. Data are collected for total employment, job openings, hiring, employees quitting, layoffs and discharges, and other separations.

Kansas City Fed Manufacturing Survey

Released on the last Thursday of each month

The Federal Reserve Bank of Kansas City surveys roughly 300 manufacturing plants that are representative of the district's industrial and geographic makeup. Indices are calculated by subtracting the percentage of total respondents reporting decreases in a given indicator from the percentage of those reporting increases. The indices, which can range from 100 to -100, reveal the general direction of the indicators by showing how, or if, the number of plants with improving conditions offset those with worsening conditions. Index values greater than zero generally suggest expansion, while values less than zero indicate contraction.

Manufacturing ISM Report on Business

Released on the first business day of each month

This report is based on data compiled from purchasing and supply executives nationwide across multiple industries. According to ISM, a reading above 50 percent indicates expansion in manufacturing, while a reading below 50 percent indicates a general decline.

Manufacturing and Trade Inventories and Sales Report

Released around the fifteenth of each month

This U.S. Census Bureau report includes distributive trade sales and manufacturers' shipments (sales); manufacturers' and trade inventories (inventories); and total business inventories/sales ratio. Estimates are based on data from three surveys: the Monthly Retail Trade Survey, the Monthly Wholesale Trade Survey, and the Manufacturers' Shipments, Inventories, and Orders Survey.

Monster.com Employment Index

Released during the first week of each month

The Monster.com Employment Index is a comprehensive monthly analysis of online job demand from Monster Worldwide, Inc. This index provides a snapshot of online recruitment nationwide.

Monthly Mass Layoffs

Released around the twentieth to the twenty-third of each month

Mass layoff statistics are compiled by the Bureau of Labor Statistics from initial unemployment insurance claims. Each month, states report on establishments that have at least 50 initial unemployment insurance claims filed against them during a consecutive five-week period, regardless of duration. These establishments then are contacted by the state agency to determine whether these separations lasted 31 days or longer, and, if so, other information concerning the layoff is collected. Quarterly mass layoff reports include additional information. The report lists how many layoff events occurred and how many people who are eligible to receive unemployment compensation were affected. Layoff events are segmented by state and industry.

Monthly Retail Trade and Food Services

Released around the twelfth of each month

This report from the U.S. Census Bureau provides an early estimate of monthly sales for retail and food service in the U.S. The survey is based on questionnaires sent to approximately 5,000 firms.

Monthly Treasury Statement

Released mid-month each month

The U.S. Department of Treasury budget is a monthly account of the surplus or deficit of the U.S. government. Detailed information is provided on receipts and outlays of the federal government. The information is provided on a monthly and fiscal year-to-date basis.

Mortgage Bankers Association's Weekly Mortgage Applications Survey

Released each Wednesday

The Mortgage Bankers Association's (MBA) Weekly Applications Survey analyzes mortgage application activity. The survey is used as an indicator of housing and mortgage finance activity.

NAHB/Wells Fargo Housing Market Index

Released mid-month each month

This index is based on a monthly survey of National Association of Home Builders (NAHB) members on the single-family housing market. The survey asks respondents to rate current market conditions for the sale of new homes and conditions in the next six months, as well as the traffic of prospective buyers.

New Home Sales

Released around the twenty-third to the twenty-fifth of each month

The Bureau of the Census compiles data for this report from sample surveys. The report includes sales figures and median prices of housing.

New Residential Construction

Released on the third Thursday of each month

New Residential Construction, released by the Bureau of the Census, provides statistics on the construction of new privately owned residential structures in the United States. Data include the number of new housing units authorized by building permits; the number of housing units authorized to be built, but not yet started; the number of housing units started; the number of housing units under construction; and the number of housing units completed.

Non-Manufacturing ISM Report on Business

Released on the third business day of each month

This index is based on data compiled from purchasing and supply executives nationwide. The index based on four indicators: business activity, new orders, employment, and supplier deliveries. According to ISM, an index reading above 50 percent indicates that the non-manufacturing economy in that index is generally expanding; below 50 percent indicates that it is generally declining. For supplier deliveries, a reading above 50 percent indicates slower deliveries and below 50 percent indicates faster deliveries.

NY Fed Empire State Manufacturing Survey

Released mid-month each month

This report is based on a monthly survey of manufacturers in New York State conducted by the Federal Reserve Bank of New York.

Personal Income

Released around the first or last business day of each month

The Personal Income report from the Bureau of Economic Analysis mainly measures the income received by households from employment, self-employment, investments, and transfer payments. It also includes small amounts for expenses of nonprofit organizations and income of certain fiduciary activities. The largest component of personal income is wages and salaries from employment. Personal income is released after the employment report and thus can be estimated by the payroll and earnings data for the employment report. Disposable income refers to personal income after the payment of income, estate, certain other taxes, and payments to governments.

Philadelphia Fed Business Outlook Survey

Released mid-month each month

Every month, the Federal Reserve Bank of Philadelphia surveys respondents to assess general business conditions as well as company business conditions. Answers are given based in the current month versus the previous month, and the outlook for six months from the current month. An indicator is presented for a decrease, no change, an increase, and a diffusion index.

Producer Price Index (PPI)

Released during the third week of each month

The Producer Price Index (PPI) from the Bureau of Labor Statistics is a family of indices that measures average changes in selling prices received by domestic producers for their output. The PPI tracks changes in prices for nearly every goods-producing industry in the domestic economy, including agriculture, electricity and natural gas, forestry, fisheries, manufacturing, and mining.

Productivity and Costs

Released quarterly, at the beginning of the month

Productivity and associated costs, compiled by the Bureau of Labor Statistics, reflects the relationship between real output and the labor and capital inputs involved in production. This shows changes over time in the amount of goods and services produced per unit of input.

Retail Sales

(See Monthly Retail Trade and Food Services)

Richmond Fed Survey of Manufacturing Activity

Released at the end of each month

The Federal Reserve Bank of Richmond surveys manufacturing plants that are representative of the district's industrial and geographic make-up. The indices are calculated by subtracting the percentage of total respondents reporting decreases in a given indicator from the percentage of those reporting increases. The indices, which can range from 100 to -100, reveal the general direction of the indicators by showing how the number of plants with improving conditions offset those with worsening conditions. Index values greater than zero generally suggest expansion, while values less than zero indicate contraction.

Semiconductor Book-to-Bill Ratio

Released around the fifteenth to the twentieth of each month

Semiconductor Equipment and Materials International releases the results of a survey of U.S. manufacturers on a monthly basis. The 3-month moving average of shipments and new orders plus their ratio, named the book-to-bill ratio, are all included.

Semiconductor Billing

First of last day of the month

The Semiconductor Industry Association reports the global dollar volume of integrated circuit sales on a three-month moving average on a monthly basis. All types of semiconductor chips are included in the totals: microprocessors, memory, and others. The sales are reported individually for four regions: North America, Asia-Pacific, Japan, and Europe. The data are compiled from a survey of the largest global chip manufacturers.

Thomson Reuters/University of Michigan Survey of Consumers

Released on the first or last day of each month

The Thomson Reuters/University of Michigan Consumer Sentiment Survey is based upon a nationally representative sample of consumer households. It reports an index of consumer sentiment and an index of consumer expectations.

Treasury Budget

(see Monthly Treasury Statement)

Unemployment Insurance Weekly Claims Report

Released each Thursday

This weekly report from the Department of Labor measures the number of applicants filing for state jobless benefits. The report is important as an indicator of employment and, therefore, economic trends. An increase in jobless claims, for example, shows that job prospects are worsening (or at least have not improved), while a decrease in claims indicates job growth. On a week-to-week basis, the claims number can be volatile. Therefore, looking at jobless claims over a longer time period (such as month-to-month) may be more meaningful.

Unemployment Rate

Released on the first Friday of each month

The unemployment rate is released by the Bureau of Labor Statistics, and represents the number unemployed as a percent of the labor force. Persons are classified as unemployed if they do not have a job, have actively looked for work in the prior four weeks, and are currently available for work. Actively looking for work may consist of any of the following activities: networking, contacting an employer directly, or having a job interview with public or private employment agency; contacting a school or university employment center; sending out resumes or filling out applications; placing or answering advertisements; checking union or professional registers; or some other means of active job search. People are counted as employed if they did any work at all for pay or profit during the survey week. This includes all part-time and temporary work, as well as regular full-time year-round employment. Persons also are counted as employed if they have a job at which they did not work during the survey week because they were on vacation, experiencing child-care problems, taking care of some other family or personal obligation, on maternity or paternity leave; involved in an industrial dispute; or prevented from working by bad weather.

Vehicle Sales

Released during the first week of each month

Auto companies report vehicle sales each month. Light vehicle sales are divided between cars and light trucks (sport utility vehicles, pickup trucks, and vans). Light vehicle sales include both sales of vehicles assembled in North America that are sold in the United States and sales of imported vehicles sold in the United States.

Weekly Natural Gas Storage Report

Released each Thursday

This report from the U.S. Energy Information Administration provides data on working gas in underground storage in the lower 48 states, including current storage and historic comparisons.

Wells Fargo/Gallup Investor and Retirement Optimism Index

Released quarterly

The index draws from investors randomly selected from across the country. An investor is defined as a person who is head of a household or a spouse in a household with total savings and investments of $10,000 or more. The sample size is comprised of roughly two-thirds non-retired people and one-third retirees.

Wholesale Trade

Released around the tenth of each month

Companies provide data to the Bureau of Census on dollar-values of merchant wholesale sales, end-of-month inventories, and methods of inventory valuation. Monthly wholesale trade, sales, and inventories reports are released six weeks after the close of the reference month. They contain preliminary current month figures and final figures for the previous month. Statistics include sales, inventories, and stock or sale ratios. Data are collected from selected wholesale firms. The sample is updated every quarter to add new businesses and eliminate those who are no longer active wholesalers.

ECONOMIC CALENDAR

Monday	Tuesday	Wednesday	Thursday	Friday
	1	**2**	**3**	**4**
	Semiconductor Billings 1	Vehicle Sales - AutoData 1	Chain Store Sales 3	Employment Situation 5
	Challenger Report 2	MBA Mortgage Applications Survey 1	Monster Employment Index 2	ECRI Weekly Leading Index 1
	Construction Spending 2	Conference Board Measure of CEO confidence 2	Jobless Claims 4	
	Manufacturing ISM Index 3		Productivity and Costs 3	
	ICSC - Goldman Sachs chain store sales 2		Factory Orders 2	
	Personal Income 3		Non-Mfg. ISM Index 4	
			Oil and Gas Inventories 2	
			Weekly Natural Gas Storage Report 2	
7	**8**	**9**	**10**	**11**
Consumer Credit 1	Chain Store Sales ICSC Goldman Sachs 2	MBA Mortgage Applications Survey 2	Jobless Claims 4	ECRI Weekly Leading Index 1
Conference Board Employment Trends Index 2		Job Openings and Labor Turnover Survey 2	Import and Export Prices 2	
		Wholesale Trade (MWTR) 3	Weekly Natural Gas Storage Report 2	
		Oil and Gas Inventories 2	Treasury Budget 3	

Scale: 1 – Least Significant; 3 – Signficant; 5 – Highly Signficant

79

Monday	Tuesday	Wednesday	Thursday	Friday
14 Retail Sales (MARTS) **3** International Trade **2**	**15** ICSC GOldman Sachs Chain Store Sales Snapshot **2** Consumer Price Index **3** Business Inventories (MTIS) **2** NY Empire State Manufacturing Survey **2** NAHB Wells Fargo Housing Market Index **2** Manufacturing and Trade Inventories and sales **2**	**16** MBA Mortgage Applications Survey **2** Industrial Production **2** Oil and Gas Inventories **2** Beige Book **4**	**17** Jobless Claims **4** The Conference Board Leading Indicators **1** Weekly Natural Gas Storage Report **2** Philadelphia Fed Survey **2** SEMI Book-to-Bill Ratio **2** New Residential Construction **1**	**18** Current Account **3** ECRI Weekly Leading Index **1** Producer Price Index **3**
21	**22** ICSC Goldman Sachs Chain Store Sales **2**	**23** MBA Mortgage Applications Survey **2** Monthly Mass Layoffs **3** Oil and Gas Inventories **2**	**24** Jobless Claims **4** Durable Goods **3** The Conference Board Help Wanted **2** New Home Sales **2** Weekly Natural Gas Storage Report **2** Kansas City Fed Manufacturing Survey **2**	**25** GDP **5** Existing Home Sales **2** ECRI Weekly Leading Index **1**

Scale: 1 – Least Significant; 3 – Signficant; 5 – Highly Signficant

Monday	Tuesday	Wednesday	Thursday	Friday
28 Personal Income **3** Wells Fargo/ Gallup Investor Optimism and Retirement **1** Richmond Fed Manufacturing Survey **2**	**29** ISCS Goldman Sachs Chain Store Sales **2** The Conference Board Consumer Confidence **3** Agricultural Prices **2**	**30** MBA Mortgage Applications Survey **2** Chicago Fed National Activity Index **2** Chicago PMI **2** Oil and Gas Inventories **2** Thomson Reuters/ University of Michigan Survey of Consumers **3**		

Scale: 1 – Least Significant; 3 – Signficant; 5 – Highly Signficant

RATINGS EXPLANATION

1 and 2 — This data is marked as the "least significant" because data release has little (if any) impact on the markets and is not a key measurement of the U.S. economy. Data marked with 1 or 2 has no role in Astor's economic model.

3 — Data given the "significant" rating indicates that the data release has a limited impact on the markets, but may represent a key area of our economy. Data marked as 3 do not have a direct impact on Astor's economic model, but are closely monitored.

4 and 5 — A "highly significant" rating indicates that the data is the most important to the market and represents a key component of the economy. Data that has a rating of 4 or 5 have a large influence on

This book, and other great products, are available at significantly discounted prices. They make great gifts for your customers, clients, and staff. For more information on these long-lasting, cost-effective premiums, please call (800) 272-2855, or email us at sales@traderslibrary.com.